Contents

Acknowledgements

I have received information and help at the British Library and Colindale, at the Wellcome Medical Institute, at Tunbridge Wells Reference Library and Museum, the Kirkstall Abbey Museum at Leeds, and the Sheffield Library, at the Bristol Library, at the Mansell Collection, at the Towner Art Gallery at Eastbourne, at the Public Baths, St Marylebone, and at the British Film Institute. To all the helpful members of staff I extend my thanks.

I have received information from archivists at Cambridge, Gosport, and Newport (Isle of Wight), and from Mr Fuller, archivist of the Sun Alliance and London Insurance Group, from W.J. Pimm of the R.S.P.C.A. and from David Godfrey, Newspaper Antiquarian, from the Friends Historical Association of the Society of Friends, from the Shaftesbury Society, and from others who possessed material concerned with the Climbing Boy.

I am indebted to the Editors of *Punch* and *The Times*.

I am grateful to many writers who have touched on the story of the Climbing Boy in their books. In particular I thank Eric Crozier for permission to quote from his libretto to Benjamin Britten's *The Little Sweep* and I would add Mrs Mary Hopkirk, author of *Nobody Wanted Sam*, Mrs L. Burton, editor of *Gosport Records,* who have provided information. Dr George Phillips of California, a world authority on chimney-sweeps, has been generous in giving me his books on climbing boys and providing me with much information in his correspondence. Advice and help have been given me by Dulcie Ashdown, Phoebe Sholto Douglas, A.P. Friend, Peter Lindley, the late Catherine Lucas, Brian Parsons, R.G.E. Sandbach, Alan S. Watts, and Madeleine West. I am grateful to Philip Miller, architect, who provided information about chimneys; and to Jim Parr of Radio Brighton, for producing five programmes on climbing boys.

I thank photographers for permission to reproduce their work: Michael Wheeler (Tunbridge Wells) and David L. White (Newport, I.O.W.).

Climbing Boys
A STUDY OF SWEEPS' APPRENTICES, 1773–1875

One hundred and two years have elapsed since the good Jonas Hanway brought the brutal iniquity before the public.

LORD SHAFTESBURY, *Diary,* 28 April 1875

Climbing Boys

A STUDY OF SWEEPS' APPRENTICES
1773–1875

K.H. STRANGE

ALLISON & BUSBY
London/New York

First published 1982 by
Allison and Busby Limited
6a Noel Street, London W1V 3RB,
England
and distributed in the USA by
Schocken Books Inc
200 Madison Avenue, New York,
NY 10016

British Library Cataloguing in Publication Data

Strange, Kathleen
  The climbing boys
  1. Chimney-sweeps – History
  2. Apprentices – History
  I. Title
  331.5'5   HD 8039.C482

  ISBN 0-85031-431-3

Design: John Latimer Smith
Set in 11/12pt Bembo by
Alan Sutton Publishing Limited
and printed in Great Britain by
Biddles Ltd, Guildford and King's Lynn

I acknowledge the help I have received from Jackdaw Publications Ltd (Jackdaw 7: Shaftesbury and the Working Children), from John Jaques firm (Tenniel's "Happy Families") and from the Philatelic Bureau.

I am grateful to Stella Irwin and to the proof-readers Kenneth Pengelly and Gillian Beaumont, and I apologize to any who have helped me and whose names do not appear on this page. To all who have shown interest in the story of the almost-forgotten victim of the Industrial Revolution, the Chimney-Sweep's Climbing Boy, I give my warmest thanks.

K.H. STRANGE

Note on
SAVE THE CHILDREN
Fund

Because I believe that there are many children throughout the world who are in this last quarter of the twentieth century suffering as much as the climbing boys suffered, and because the "Save the Children" Fund (157 Clapham Road, London SW9) aims to seek them out and remove their sufferings, I am asking the organizers of the Fund to accept royalties from the sales of this book.

The unremitting efforts of the Friends of the Climbing Boys brought their climbs eventually to an end; I believe the unremitting efforts of the Friends of Children Everywhere will reduce hunger and disease and heartbreaking conditions.

K.H.S.

List of Illustrations

Introduction

For the grin of a sweep hath absolutely no malice in it.
CHARLES LAMB

This book is not all horror, soot and brutality. There are some lighter touches breaking through, like the white-toothed smile on a sweep's soot-engrained face.

Mention *sweep* to adults and they will remember with pleasure their early introduction to Tom, the climbing boy turned water-baby. Mention *sweep* to a child and there will be an instant connection with Mary Poppins or Hans Christian Andersen's story. Don't we all smile at a sweep, or raise our hats to him? We are as delighted to see him on our wedding-day as if he were a black cat: good luck and happiness are forecast for the couple.

The last chapter of this book is called "Climbing Boys in Art and Literature". The idea for this is borrowed from the remarkable book of 1824, *The Chimney-Sweeper's Friend and Climbing-Boy's Album,* compiled by James Montgomery. Like that writer, I wanted to produce a book for people who are interested in life all around them and who like to link it with the past and the future.

How similar and how dissimilar were the lives of our parents and our grandparents to ours? And how are things shaping for our children and our grandchildren (in my case, my great-nephews and great-nieces)? My own parents were born before the last climbing boy perished on his job; my grandparents lived during the time when boys were being sent up chimneys "with the full knowledge and consent of thousands of all classes".

This book has evolved over a period of time. It started in the autumn of 1974 when, sitting in a park in Newport, Isle of Wight, I saw a memorial to a boy, Valentine Gray, who had died in 1822 at the age of ten. He was a sweep's climbing boy, and has led me into the world of the nine-teenth century: into the House of Commons and the House of Lords, into workhouses and orphanages and baby-farms, into the industrial north and London, into palatial homes like Mrs Montagu's in Portman Square and into "rookeries" of unbelievable stench and squalor not a mile away. That boy has encouraged me to read old copies of *Punch* and *The Times,* Dickens and Kingsley, Jonas Hanway and James Montgomery, William Blake and Charles Lamb, Sir Edwin Chadwick and Henry Mayhew. He has introduced me to a number of interesting historical people – some of whom I had barely heard of before – and has taken me in imagination to many places remote from my usual environment.

Valentine Gray, aged ten, has shown me the world he lived in and has drawn my attention to the fact that influential people with God and justice and intelligence on their side may have to endure years of apparent defeat.

This book covers the half-century before Valentine's death in 1822, and just over the half-century after it: 1773–1875. In 1773 appeared Jonas Hanway's *State of Chimney-Sweepers' Young Apprentices;* in 1875 occurred the last record of a boy's death caused by climbing a chimney.

Valentine Gray has posed the question to me: had I lived in the nineteenth century, would I have joined the campaign for superseding the employment of climbing boys? Would I have brought a sweep to court for breaking the law? Would I have presented a sweeping-machine to a sweep on condition that he discharged his boy? Would I have "rescued" a boy and brought him up? Would I?

I do not answer the questions direct because I do not know; but my note about the Save the Children fund will explain to my readers that I am answering the questions obliquely by helping in a campaign for the children of the world who are suffering in the times in which we live. It was the son of a sweep who used to clean my chimneys who reminded me that the past is over and done with: it is the present and future which matter.

Finally, before you read this book, will you cut out a nine-inch square of cardboard and remind yourself that *that* is the size of many of the flues up which the climbing boy – the "chummy" – was forced to climb; and draw a seven-inch square on it: it is on record that a six-year-old girl went up a seven-inch flue.

Chronology 1773–1875

This table sets out dates of importance in the study of climbing boys, and supplements them with details of some other events of importance to child welfare and social reform.

The first and last dates are taken from an entry in Lord Shaftesbury's diary of 28 April 1875: "One hundred and two years have elapsed since the good Jonas Hanway brought the brutal iniquity before the public . . . ."

Earlier than 1773 there had been some written reports, and Jonas Hanway, that "espouser of good causes", had published revelations on the subject in 1763 and 1765, and had also published his recommendations for the formation of Friendly Societies for Master-Sweeps.

PRIVATE INITIATIVE	PUBLIC REGULATION
1773 Publication of Jonas Hanway's *State of Chimney Sweepers' Young Apprentices.*	1774 Building Act containing *inter alia* recommendations on construction of chimneys.
1785 Publication of Jonas Hanway's *Sentimental History of Chimney Sweeps in London and Westminster.*	
1788 Publication of James Andrews' *Appeal to the Humane on Behalf of Climbing Boys.*	1788 Chimney Sweepers' Act.
1789 William Blake's *Songs of Innocence.*	
1792 Publication of David Porter's *Considerations on the Present State of Chimney Sweepers.*	
1796 Formation of the Society for Bettering the Conditions and Increasing the Comforts of the Poor.	
1798 Sunday School for climbing boys at Kingston-on-Thames.	
1800 Society for the Protection and Instruction of Chimney Sweep Apprentices (this lasted only one year).	1802 Act on Health and Morals of Apprentices.
1803 Society for the Encouraging of Arts, Manufacture and Commerce set competition for chimney-cleaning machine: won by George Smart. Society's Gold Medal awarded to Smart.	
1803 Founding of the first Society for Superseding the Employment of Climbing Boys.	1816 Petitions to Parliament by the

Society for Superseding.
1817/1818/1819
Select Committees appointed
by Parliament to investigate
practice of employing climbing boys.
Bill recommending abolition
of practice passed by
Commons, rejected by
Lords.
1819/1820/1825/1830
Factory and other Acts concerning child labour and
1822 Charles Lamb's essay, "In   other labour.
Praise of Chimney Sweepers".
1824 James Montgomery's *Chimney-Sweeper's Friend and Climbing Boy's Album.*
1826 Formation of the United
Society of Master Sweeps, to
fight reformers.
1828 John Glass's improved
sweeping-machine put on the
market; approved by Fire
Insurance companies and
others.
1829 Society for Superseding published *Observations on the
Cruelty of employing climbing
boys.*   1832 Reform Bill, with extension
of franchise.
1832 Ashley Cooper (later Lord
Shaftesbury) appointed by
Parliament adviser on child
welfare.
1833 Abolition of Slave Trade in
the British Empire.
1833 Factory Act.
1834 Chimney Sweep Act. An
apprentice must be "willing
and desirous".
1834 Building Act of 1774 amended.
Regulations on chimneys and
flue construction.
1834/37/38
Poor Law Commission. Poor
Law Amendment Act. Sec-
retary: Edwin Chadwick.
1837 Accession of Queen Victoria.
1838 Publication of Dickens's 1840 Select Committee to examine
Oliver Twist.   effects of Factory Act of
1833.

1840 Act for Regulation of Chimney Sweeps and Chimneys.

1842 Publication of Chadwick's report on Sanitary Conditions of the Labouring Population of Great Britain: "It is an awful document not to be read without a feeling of shame, terror and indignation" (Shaftesbury).

1842 Mines Act: exclusion of children under 10 from mines.

1844 Foundation of the Ragged School Union. Formation of Society for Improving Conditions of the Labouring Classes.

1846 Public Baths and Washhouses Act.

1847 Ten Hours Act passed, limiting children's labour to 10 hours *per diem*.

1848 First Public Health Act.

1850 Select Committee report on Chimney Sweeps. Other Acts: Factory; Coal Mines Inspection.

1851 Henry Mayhew's *London Labour and the London Poor.*

1851/52 Shaftesbury presented Bills to Parliament, unsuccessful.

1863 Children's Employment Commission appointed. New Bill recommended.

1864 Chimney Sweeps Regulation Act, prohibiting employment of children under 16 years as chimney sweeps.

1863 Charles Kingsley's *Water Babies.*

1860/1864/1874 Several Acts concerning Factories; Labourers' Dwellings; Fire Brigades; Workshops.

1870 Education Act making education compulsory for all children.

1874/75 Factory Act; Artisans and Labouring Dwellings Improvement Act; Public Health Act.

1875 Death of George Brewster, aged 11, climbing boy at Fulbourn near Cambridge.

1875 Lord Shaftesbury's final Bill passed. Annual licence for chimney-sweeps to be enforced.

CHAPTER 1
The Climbing Boy's World 1773–1875

A most important matter it is, to put paupers in the way of ceasing
to be paupers.
WILLIAM COBBETT, *Diary*, August 1 1823

There they were – six young children in nice clean clothes, with a
filthy little blackamoor lying in the fireplace and sobbing as though
his heart would break. All they could get out of him was "Please
don't send me up again!" Over and over again he said it.
ERIC CROZIER, libretto for Benjamin Britten's
Let's Make an Opera! (1949)

Throughout the great ages of human achievement . . . the mass of
voiceless people have had a hard time. Poverty, hunger, plagues,
disease: they were the background of history right up to the end of
the nineteenth century, and most people regarded them as inevitable
– like bad weather.
LORD CLARK, *Civilization*, chapter 13
– Heroic Materialism (1969)

A century and two years: a period mentioned by Lord
Shaftesbury as one of special significance in the history of
chimney-sweeps. 1773 is the year when Jonas Hanway
launched his campaign – after preliminary attempts – for
better conditions for sweeps' climbing boys. 1875 is the year
when the combined forces of Parliament and numerous
campaigners brought to an end the long and dangerous
climb of sweeps' apprentices; it is the year when the last boy
died as a result of chimney climbing. In 1773 the Industrial
Revolution, precursor of the Victorian Age, is gaining
momentum; a hundred and two years later the Victorian
Age itself is half over.

There is today a growing awareness, perhaps an increasing appreciation, of the Victorian Age. In Queen Victoria's
day the British Empire was still expanding and the country
prospered. Was this the period forecast by Milton:
"Methinks I see in my mind a noble and puissant nation
rousing herself like a strong man after sleep, and shaking her
invincible locks . . ."? Or was it the period depicted by the

artist Cruikshank showing a triangle with Queen Victoria forming the pinnacle, and "the lower orders" forming the base as a support to all the classes of society from royalty downwards? On this bottom row stands the chimney-sweep in company with other members of the unskilled labouring classes.

It was in Victoria's time that England found herself changing from a predominantly rural nation to an urban one: when steam-power, to take one example, was revolutionizing the way of life of millions of people; if this had not been so the climbing boy's story would have taken a different course.

Because of steam-power, mills were being built in great numbers for the purpose of producing speedily and in quantity what the hand-loom weavers had been creating slowly and in limited quantity. Hand-loom weavers found themselves out of work, they grew more and more impoverished, and those living near the expanding industrial areas found no alternative but to send their children to the mills to earn at least something. Out of the question to choose the workhouse: only total despair would take self-respecting people there.

Before the nineteenth century the subject of child labour was hardly one that received much attention. Parents claimed control of their children and could treat them as it suited them – even sell them if driven to that by poverty. The children of artisan and rural labouring classes grew up seeing life in terms of work, guided by their parents. As the nineteenth century progressed, they were to find that working for employers was a very different matter from working for parents. The children of the upper classes received tuition as befitted the class into which destiny had put them: it was unthinkable that they should go out to work, to earn wages. "The rich man in his castle, the poor man at his gate" are lines of a hymn which were valid during the Victorian era but are expurgated today.

A paragraph in Edwin Hodder's *Life and Work of the Seventh Earl of Shaftesbury, K.G.* (1886) refers to "the legalized slavery to which the children were subjected, in connection with employment in earthenware, porcelain, hosiery, pin and needle making, manufacture of arms, iron works and forges, iron foundries, glass trade, collieries, calico printing, tobacco manufacture, button factories, bleaching and paper mills, and various other industries . . .". No inspectors, no social workers to find fault or advise, no one to help solve problems; in fact, no interference. The end-product of the children's work was accepted without question by the public: out of sight was out of mind.

It was mainly Lord Shaftesbury, appointed by Parliament in 1832 as adviser and leader for child welfare, who brought facts to light. From his position, near the top of Cruikshank's triangle, he was able to see the whole scene. By 1840 he was writing in his *Diary:*

> Jews, chimney-sweeps, factory children, education, church extension etc. etc.: I shall succeed, I fear, partially in all, and completely in none. Yet we must persevere. . . .

In December in the same year he contributed an article on "Infant Labour" in the influential *Quarterly Review,* and the astonished readers learned of the thousands of children working at unskilled jobs in a great variety of trades for fifteen and more hours daily; one of Lord Shaftesbury's aims was to spread information about the subjects which he was painfully discovering for himself.

Where did all these children come from? Impoverished parents and penniless widows handed them over; so did orphanages in order to save on the children's upkeep. Orphanage children had a terrifyingly high death-rate, but those who survived were sent off in droves to the dark Satanic mills of the industrial north.

The work of the labouring classes of 1760 to 1832 – the seventy-odd years before Lord Shaftesbury's appointment – is summarized in two books by J.L. and Barbara Hammond: *The Village Labourer* (1911) and *The Town Labourer* (1917); later they wrote *Lord Shaftesbury* (1923) and just one extract from the last book is revealing. Returns for 1835 showed that 28,000 children *under thirteen* were working in cotton-mills in a total work-force of 220,000; 9,000 children in wool factories, in a total work-force of 55,000; and 4,000 children in worsted factories, in a total work-force of 16,000. Thus 41,000 children under thirteen – one-seventh of the total number of workers – were employed in mills. They were set to work at tedious, harmful, exhausting tasks. Undernourished, ill-housed, uneducated, deprived of normal rest and exercise and fun, how would such children grow up,

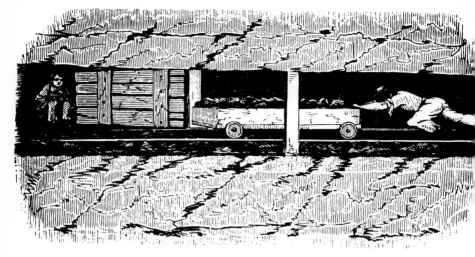

if, that is, they survived?

Could work in the mines be worse than in the mills? Children of only a few years of age were taken underground to do repetitive jobs in the dark and they suffered illnesses, deformities and mental disturbance as a result. An illustrated report was published in 1842. Perhaps the illustrations made more impression than the figures given. One picture showed two children, one a six-year-old boy sitting in the dark in a wall-bay, his job being to open and close a trap-door for coal trucks to pass through; the other a boy pushing the loaded truck and stooping under the three-foot-high roof. Both boys would be working a shift for hours on end. A picture which occasioned a still greater shock was that showing a boy and girl, nearly naked, being lowered by rope down a mine-shaft, each sitting on the same narrow bar and clutching the rope.

The factories and the mines swallowed up the children in ever greater numbers. Factories were growing in number and size, mines were being extended, to keep pace with expanding trade at home and abroad. The cheap labour of children helped provide the profits of manufacturers and mine-owners. At the same time towns were expanding in size: London was growing fast, so were the ports, so were the industrial and mining towns of the north and midlands. Bigger towns – more and bigger houses – more and longer chimneys – this expansion brings us to a third category of labouring children: the climbing boys employed by chimney-sweepers, the children who are the subject of this book.

Did they really climb nine-inch flues, flues that twisted and turned in the dark, flues that were burning hot, flues that ended in dangerous chimney-stacks which, disintegrating, could send the climber crashing to the pavement below? Did the boys really get sold or "lent" and did they "sleep black"? Did their indentures as apprentices mean almost nothing? If the answer is "yes" to any or all of these questions, how had this come about?

The story of the chimney needs to be studied before we can understand why the period mentioned by Lord Shaftesbury, 1773–1875, is selected for recording the black history of climbing boys.

During the last half of the seventeenth century and throughout the eighteenth there was a rapid growth of the brick–built town house; the disastrous Great Fire of London

Above and left: two illustrations of children in mines, from First Report of the Children's Employment Commission in Mines and Manufacturers, 1842.

in 1666 led to an Act regulating the rebuilding of the city. This governed the construction of buildings, the thickness of brickwork, the size of timber scantlings and the ceiling heights in multi-storeyed houses. Coal was being increasingly used as a substitute for wood – the use of which had led to severe reductions in the size of the great forests – and a tax on coal helped to raise money for public buildings. Coal required a good draught and fireplaces were designed accordingly and flues were reduced in size. Smaller flues became blocked with soot and this not only limited efficiency but also tended to result in disastrous fires if the chimneys were not swept regularly. The larger flues in the older houses were not difficult to clean by the owner or his servants.

In 1774, and again in 1834 and 1840, Building Acts were passed for the regulation of buildings and chimneys with instructions about regular sweeping.

Smart's sweeping-machine, invented for the purpose of sweeping the longer and narrower flues, was on the market in 1803. Already sweeps had been sending small boys up flues to clean them and the machine was intended to supersede this employment. Smart's machine was suitable for straightforward flues with no right-angle bends (where soot collected), but was less useful in some flues such as those in public buildings and royal palaces: as many as fourteen changes of direction, *including downwards,* could be traced on building plans.

The Surveyor-General of the Board of Works, B.C. Stephenson, made extensive investigations in public buildings and recommended Smart's machine, and others which were "simple, repairable and portable". Then in 1826 J.W. Hiort, Chief Examiner in His Majesty's Office of Works and Public Buildings, published a *Practical Treatise on the Construction of Chimneys;* this demonstrated what Stephenson had indicated: that the practice of employing boys was unnecessary and that a well-designed chimney would function efficiently with a nine-inch by nine-inch flue. He did not approve of pots, cowls and "whimsical contrivances" on chimney stacks: prevention of trouble was better than elaborate attempts to cure.

Other sweeping-machines came on the market and were advertised in leaflets and such publications as *The Mechanics'*

Magazine. This last published on 14 October 1826 a detailed drawing of a machine designed by T.B. of Sun Tavern Field, London, with an explanatory text about the combination of rollers, hinges, wheels on small rods, weights and fans and vertical rod with brushes attached: the contrivance adapted itself to flues of varying widths. Then in 1828 Joseph Glass, a former master-sweep, designed a machine which was an improvement in flexibility on those in use; he claimed that he could sweep almost any flue in eight minutes or less, and that his machine was suitable for chimneys in the Houses of Parliament, most of those in Buckingham Palace, and those in tall houses of eighty feet. He affirmed that "any flues not fit for the machine were not fit for a boy" – an affirmation that some master-sweeps would not accept. Joseph Glass recommended access doors to the flue and these could be made inexpensively and "without damage even in the best drawing-room".

In *The Mechanics' Magazine* of 4 October 1834 Joseph Glass wrote an article on chimney-sweeping, illustrating it with a remarkable drawing of a seven-flue chimney stack in section. Here is his description of the flues, which are labelled A to G:

> *A* represents a chimney with two right angles (and) a climbing boy stuck fast in the horizontal part of the flue, with his head buried in soot. Scores of climbing boys have thus lost their lives. *B* – a climbing-boy in the attitude in which he ascends chimneys. *C* – a climbing boy brushing out the chimney-pot. *E* – a climbing boy stuck fast, with his knees up to his chin – he can neither get up nor down. Boys have been stuck fast for hours in this way, and have notwithstanding survived, as their position did not affect their breathing. *G* – a chimney with the angles rounded off, and adapted to the machine. . . .

Yet another sweeping-machine was invented by the Brighton architect Amon Henry Wilds, who lodged a patent in 1843 for a machine capable of cleaning horizontal chimney flues. A Cambridge sweep invented an adaptable machine holding four brushes, not two (a sample is on show in the Cambridge Folk Museum); he was awarded a medal by the Cambridge Climbing Boys' Association for his attempt to replace the climbing boy.

The student of chimneys will remark the change that has

taken place in the second half of the twentieth century: new forms of heating, the creation of smokeless zones, the decline of open fires, all mean less work for sweeps and housewives. Soot, valuable as a fertilizer, has become scarce. Where chimneys are still swept the form of brush based on Glass's early invention is still used by many sweeps. But the sweeps do not apprentice small boys to do the work. The historian can unfold an elaborate story concerning people and buildings by starting with a hole in the roof, and providing details about the period up to 1875 when small boys, and a few small girls, shinned up soot-engrimed chimneys.

He can amplify the story by investigating the history of fire-fighting and fire-insurance. Climbing boys were doubtless unaware of their importance in saving buildings from fire by their removal of soot, though Robert Steven could have told them.

Steven, friend of Lord Shaftesbury and champion of climbing boys, was appointed Secretary of the Hand-in-Hand Insurance Co. in 1833, and he earned high praise for his "unwearying labours". It was Robert Steven who had convinced other insurance offices that the system of using boys in chimneys was as unnecessary as it was cruel. Even before Steven's appointment the Hand-in-Hand had come out on the side of the boys, for, when the Master-Sweepers were opposing the Bill relative to climbing boys, they approached the Hand-in-Hand for a subscription towards their expenses: the answer was NO.

The historian of fire insurance could in fact write a book called *Our Debt to the Climbing Boy,* as a posthumous tribute to the thousands of boys who for over a century toiled up and down chimneys and obtained more kicks than ha'pence in their own day. Our debt will never be paid, but the "suffering innocence" of the boys, to one of whom the people of Newport, Isle of Wight, raised a memorial, deserves a place in the recorded history of fire insurance.

The climbing boy's world, the climbing boy's chimney have been sketched in this chapter as a preliminary to the stories of the boys and of their numerous champions who tried in a variety of ways to "supersede the employment of the climbing boy". There were a hundred and two years of endeavour, as Lord Shaftesbury pointed out: a hundred and two years when poets and novelists, when lords and master-sweeps, when inventors and builders, together with countless other individuals known and unknown, struggled to bring to an end the almost unbelievable employment of climbing boys.

Children are still vulnerable. It is significant that many of the child welfare organizations which function today were founded in the period covered by this book: Dr Barnardo's, the Waifs and Strays, the Shaftesbury Society, the National Society for the Prevention of Cruelty to Children – and others – came into activity because Victorian consciences pricked. Their functions differ because they have to adapt to suit changing conditions, but they indicate a continuing concern for the welfare of children.

CHAPTER 2
Apprenticeship:
Who were the Boys?

The author is anxious to declare her detestation of the newly
broached doctrine that the poor have no right to a sufficiency of
necessary food to sustain the life that God has given them. . . .
FRANCES TROLLOPE (1780–1863), *Jessie Phillips*

The poor raised families as an insurance policy for their old age, so
that they might have a roof over their heads when they were old.
The rich were interested in the continuity of their family line and
estates. . . .
Punch on Children – a Panorama 1845–1864,
published 1975 by David Duff

What was the meaning of apprenticeship in the period 1773–
1875? The idea has been the same throughout the centuries;
it means a training, a learning of a trade, with responsibility
on the part of the master to teach and of the pupil to learn.
The fact that, once he was in the chimney, a boy would
have to make his own way without anyone's help did not
invalidate the indenture.

A typical indenture is that of John Batty, aged eight: in
1825 he was apprenticed "to John Ives of Newark to learn
the trade and mystery of chimney-sweeper". The word
"mystery" used in indentures derives from the Latin word
ministerium which explains itself; but John Batty and his
friends would have chosen to derive it like the other word
"mystery", which comes from a Greek work for "close lips
or eyes", and meant, among others things, "hidden matters,
obscurity". John Batty was certainly going to find hidden
matters and obscurity in his work. John Ives undertook to
provide John Batty with a second suit of clothes, and to
have him cleansed once a week; he agreed that he might go
to church, that he would not force him up chimneys
actually on fire, and would treat him with humanity and
care as far as the employment would permit. John Batty was
forbidden "to call the streets" between 7 a.m. and noon in
winter, and 5 a.m. and noon in the summer; but there was

WILLIAM HALL,

Chimney-Sweeper and Nightman,

No. 1, SMALL-COAL ALLEY,

Near SPITAL SQUARE,

NORTON-FALGATE.

no restriction on the boy's working hours.

The words "treat him with humanity and care" admit of varied interpretation according to the interpreter: the humane and inhumane master-sweeps would have differing views. In the absence of inspectors and social workers, who was there to translate the wording of the indenture to the advantage of the boy whom it was intended to protect? Who was there to supervise Ives's method of carrying out his promise?

An indenture to be found in the Bristol City Archives is between a boy, Thomas Coles, and a sweep, William Lane. Thomas and his father sealed the document with an X and a thumb-print, William Lane wrote his signature and added his thumb-print. In some five hundred words of legal verbiage the indenture bound the boy to seven years' apprenticeship from the year 1826. By this deed, the boy would serve his master, keep his secrets and gladly carry out his commands. He would not waste or lend his master's goods, hurt his master in any way, nor haunt taverns and gaming-houses, nor "from the service of his said master day nor night . . . absent himself." For his part of the deed William Lane, having received £4 from the overseers of the poor of the parish of Pitminster, would have the boy instructed in the art of chimney-sweeping, and would allow him enough meat, drink, washing, lodging and other necessaries.

Inserting a number of legal words with which few people except lawyers could have been familiar, G.P. Hinton, Attorney at Law, Bristol, certified that he had read and explained the Deed to Thomas Coles and his father and William Lane, and they "appeared perfectly to apprehend the same."

As soon as a sweep and his new apprentice left the attorney's office they probably forgot all about the indenture. A lot of sweeps certainly did not keep the promises they made. A law had been passed as far back as 1793 providing for the punishment of masters who ill-treated their apprentices – not just climbing boys. The Newgate Calendar records great numbers of prosecutions for cruelty (there is no suggestion that master-sweeps had the monopoly of it) but obviously much cruelty was over-looked and not brought to the courts. Parliament does not terminate ill-treatment by passing an Act. One Nottingham master-sweep, called before the magistrates on a charge of cruelty, did not deny it; he took the line that some cruelty was essential and summoned one of his apprentices to confirm this. The boy did so and seemed to bear no resent-ment against his master. Another master-sweep, John Cook, gave evidence to the 1817 Select Committee. He had been a climbing boy at the age of six but would not use boys himself for climbing chimeys; he was an advocate of the machine. He gave instances of cruelty and when asked if boys showed great repugnance to climbing said that they did, and that some of them could be forced up by being told that otherwise they would go back to their parents, which might mean starvation and other hardships created by

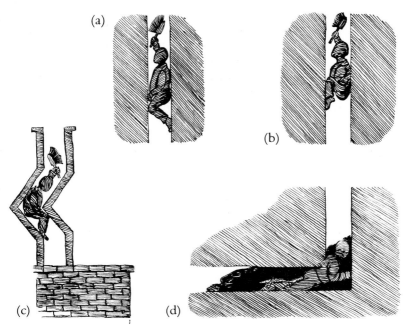

Four diagrams of boys in flues.

poverty. Another master-sweep, John Fisher, gave evidence of boys having the soles of their feet pricked to make them climb, or of having hay burnt under them.

A sign of the apprenticeship was the brass cap badge which the boy, after the Act of 1788, had to wear; it showed his master's name and address and was intended to be of some use to authority. One of these badges can be seen in the Kirkstall Abbey House Museum, Leeds.

There are numerous records setting out the practical details of "the trade and mystery of chimney sweeper". *The Climbing Boys' Advocate* of October 1856 gives the following description, explaining that this was the work before the Chimney-Sweepers' Act of 1840:

> In sweeping chimneys, the boy finds his climbing cap indispensable. He draws it over his face below his chin. It protects his eyes, nose and mouth by preventing the entrance of the soot. The cap is made of coarse cloth, and is double or threefold.

While the man is fixing the cloth (i.e. in front of the opening to the flue) the boy takes off his shoes, if he has any, and his clothes, retaining only his shirt and trousers. He passes behind the cloth and begins to ascend. With his right hand he holds his brush over his head; with his back and feet he presses the side of the flue behind him, and with his knees the side of the flue before him, and with his left arm and hand the side of the flue on his left hand, when, after the manner of the caterpillar, by successive movements, he hitches himself to the top. (a) If the chimney is fourteen inches by nine throughout, the boy can pass through with facility. On coming down, the boy slightly presses the sides of the flue, and slides down rapidly. . . . (b)

The writer continued with information as to how the boy had to manage extra wide flues, then extra narrow ones, and how to get past angles, soot blockages and other obstructions. The job sounds impossible: (c) and (d).

An even more vivid description of apprenticeship was given by a master–sweep, Ruff of Nottingham. In a statement to the Children's Employment Commission (1863) he said:

No one knows the cruelty which a boy has to undergo in learning. The flesh must be hardened. This is done by rubbing it, chiefly on the elbows and knees with the strongest brine, as that got from a pork-shop, close by a hot fire. You must stand over them with a cane, or coax them by a promise of a halfpenny, etc. if they will stand a few more rubs.

At first they will come back from their work with their arms and knees streaming with blood, and the knees looking as if the caps had been pulled off. Then they must be rubbed with brine again, and perhaps go off at once to another chimney. In some boys I have found that the skin does not harden for years.

The best age for teaching boys is about six. That is thought a nice trainable age. But I have known two at least of my neighbours' children begin at the age of five. I once saw a child only 4½ years in the market-place in his sooty clothes and with his scraper in his hand . . . he began when he was four.

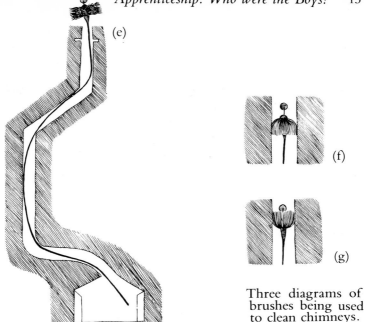

(e)

(f)

(g)

Three diagrams of brushes being used to clean chimneys.

Ruff told the Commission that he was losing customers because he would not employ boys: "I did for a time try to bring up one of my own children to it, but my wife and I felt that we could not stand it any longer, and that we would sooner go to the workhouse than suffer what we did from it."

Another master-sweep of Nottingham, Thomas Clarke, also gave some valuable information to the Commission:

It [apprenticeship] is as bad as the Negro slavery, only it is not so known. . . . I had myself formerly boys as young as 5½ years, but I did not like them; they were too weak. I was afraid they might go off. . . . They go off just as quietly as you might fall asleep in the chair, by the fire there.

I have known eight or nine sweeps lose their lives by the sooty cancer. The private parts which it seizes are entirely eaten off caused entirely by "sleeping black", and breathing the soot in all night.

He added that machines could do the work well and that he had never come across a chimney which a machine could not clean: (e), (f) and (g).

Another report on apprenticeship came from Richard Stansfield of Manchester; he himself had been a climbing boy from the age of five. He had been so cruelly treated that he ran away; his master tracked him down, and the report continues:

> And then he nearly killed me. . . . In learning a child you can't be soft with him, you must use violence. . . . We slept 5 or 6 boys together in a kind of cellar with the soot bags over us, sticking in the wounds sometimes; that and some straw were all our bed and bedclothes; they were the same bags we had used by day, wet or dry. I could read and we used sometimes to subscribe for a candle. . . .

> They are filthy in their habits, lads often wear one shirt right on till it is done with. I have been fifteen months without being washed except by the rain; why, I have been almost walking away with vermin.

When Henry Mayhew was preparing his book on *London Labour and the London Poor* he obtained his information direct from the workers. Here is a chimney-sweep living in Bethnal Green sometime in the 1840s:

> "Yes, I was a climbing boy and sarved a rigler printiceship for seven years. I was out of my printiceship when I was fourteen. Father was a silk-weaver, and did all he knew to keep me from being a sweep, but I would be a sweep, and nothink else. . . . I niver thought of anythink but climbing: it wasn't so bad at all as some people would make you believe. There are two or three ways of climbing. In wide flues you climb with your elbows and your legs spread out, your feet pressing against the sides of the flue, but in narrow flues, such as nine-inch ones, you must slant it; you must have your sides in the angles, it's widest there, and go up that way."

Here he threw himself into position — placing one arm close to his side, with the palm of the hand turned out-wards, as if pressing the side of the flue, and extending the other arm high above his head, the hand apparently pressing in the same manner.

> "There," he continued, "that's slantin'. You just put yourself in that way, and see how small you can make

yourself. I niver got to say stuck myself, but a many of them did; yes, and were taken out dead. They were smothered for want of air, and the fright, and a stayin' so long in the flue; you see the waistband of their trousers sometimes got turned down in the climbing, and in narrow flues, when not able to get it up, then they stuck."

Did the lawyers who prepared the indentures with so much legal solemnity ever find out that apprenticeship was not as set out in the indentures, but as described by the Bethnal Green sweep?

It was the master-sweeps who provided much of the general information about chimney-sweeping. Here is George Ruff of Nottingham again:

Twenty-five years ago I was the first agent in this town of an association formed to prevent the use of climbing boys. At one time soon after the Act (1840) their number in this town was brought very low. But lately they have very much increased. A few months ago I made out a list of 14 men here employing between them 21 boys; one employed three. The boys are, I should say, between the ages of 8 and 14, with a few perhaps of 6 and 7. . . . There is competition here between those who use boys and those who will not. . . . The law against climbing boys is a dead letter here. . . . Many householders will have their chimneys swept by boys instead of by machinery. I have myself lost a great amount of custom which I should otherwise have. . . . I have been sent away from magistrates' houses, and in some cases even by ladies who have professed to pity the boys.

Ruff went on to say 'that a kidnapper had "stolen" one of his boys once, in order to supply an order from France. He described also the astonishment of two journeymen whom he employed and provided with lodging: they did not expect sheets on their beds nor were they prepared to wash, but having got used to these arrangements they agreed that they liked them; three washes a year – at Whitsuntide, Goose Fair and Christmas – had sufficed them in the past.

The Commission had heard something of sooty cancer from Thomas Clarke, who had said it was caused by "sleeping black" and breathing soot in all night. Mr H.W. Lord, a member of the Commission, asked what "sleeping black" meant. It was Richard Stansfield who undertook to let him know, and we have Mr Lord's description of his visit to a sweep's house:

> I followed Stansfield down some broken stone steps into a dirty and ill-drained area in a district of Manchester, where a dense population is closely packed in small and crowded dwellings. He entered a door, and after some delay returned and took me in with him to a low-pitched unsavoury cellar, the only occupants of which appeared at first to be a woman and two little girls in ragged clothes.
>
> After some little time I discovered by the fire-light, there being no candle, a small bedstead, which with the wooden three-legged stools and a table constituted all the furniture of the place; on it was a mattress, and on the mattress a black heap, which ultimately proved to be a young man who was sleeping underneath the blanket which he used to catch the soot in his trade of chimney-sweeping.
>
> He and his blanket were both quite black, and that blanket I was told was the only bed-covering for his wife and two daughters who were then preparing to join him; I certainly could see no other.
>
> Simpson (a witness) told me that the stench there at times was enough to knock him down, and that he would never go inside, but kicked at the door and smoked his pipe outside till someone came.

All these reports, and others, show that information about the boys' employment was not withheld from those who wanted to know it. Statistics about the numbers of boys affected was also available. For instance, in 1785 Jonas Hanway estimated that in London and Westminster there were a hundred master-sweeps who employed two hundred journeymen and four hundred climbing boys, as well as fifty itinerant sweeps with their hundred and fifty boys. Seven years later David Porter, master sweep and friend of Hanway, estimated that there were two hundred master-sweeps, two hundred journeymen and five hundred boys in the same area.

In 1817 William Tooke, secretary and treasurer to the

London Society for Superseding the Employment of Climbing Boys, in evidence to the Parliamentary Commission, estimated that there were about two hundred master-sweeps in London, and about five hundred apprentices. He gave the opinion that only about twenty of the masters were reputable men who conformed to the provisions of the 1788 Act. The Commission learned that the total number of boys taken on by sweeps might be two thousand, most of them from workhouses.

When Tooke was questioned about the boys, he said that it was impossible to state how old the boys were, but that many were below the prescribed age and that the youngest and weakest were in the service of the worst type of sweeps. He confirmed that he had heard of parents selling their children, and of master-sweeps employing their own children for climbing, without apprenticing them.

By 1841, according to a statement by Henry Mayhew, author of *London Labour and the London Poor* (1851), there were 619 male and 44 female sweeps over twenty years of age, and 370 apprentices under twenty, all these in the area of London. In 1854 Lord Shaftesbury referred to "the four thousand wretched children who were at that time engaged in this disgusting and unnecessary employment". In Leicester in 1856 there were more than a hundred boys.

In 1862 the Children's Employment Commission, making investigations about the violation of the Chimney-Sweeps' Act of 1840, received reports that there were several thousand children between the ages of five and fourteen, many of them girls. It was reported to this Commission that any number of children were obtainable in Liverpool – because there were "lots of bad women there". Much of the evidence given to this Commission bore a resemblance to what had been reported to Parliament before. In addition to reports of death, hardship and degradation there were statements from different parts of the country of magistrates and police condoning the employment of boys, of the law concerning construction of chimneys being ignored, of sweeps being pressured to employ boys in order to improve their trade. It was clear, too, from statements made that, where Societies for Superseding the Employment of Climbing Boys were active, the employment of boys decreased noticeably.

But *who* were the boys? From newspapers such as *The Times*, the *Leeds Intelligencer*, the *Sheffield Iris*, the *County Herald*, the *Liverpool Mercury* and other local papers, from journals such as *Notes and Queries* and the *Annual Register*, from city archives and literary allusions, from inquiries set up by Jonas Hanway and Parliamentary Commissions, much information is obtainable about many of the boys, some of them named, some of them nameless. In many cities people formed organizations calling themselves "Society for Superseding the Employment of Climbing Boys" and one of their purposes was to collect and disseminate information about the boys employed as climbing boys. *The Climbing Boys' Advocate* was a four-page monthly periodical published from May 1856 for several years; it was produced by Judd and Company of Gray's Inn Road, London, and aimed to give publicity to all circumstances concerning climbing boys. Each issue contained articles, correspondence, accounts of meetings and proceedings in various parts of the country, including information about towns where the machine had superseded the boys.

For the most part climbing boys came from the working class, from "the lower orders"; some were no doubt the illegitimate children of middle- and upper-class people. The story of the boys is bound up with the Industrial Revolution and its aftermath.

When Pitt as Prime Minister said that children could earn their keep from the age of five years he was not alluding specifically to climbing boys; but he was referring to children of the working class only. It was stated in the Parliamentary Register of 12 February 1796 that: "Experience had already shown how much could be done by the industry of children, and the advantages of early employing them in such branches of manufacture as they are capable to execute."

Pitt was carrying responsibility for the Poor Law Amendment Bill at the time. When another Prime Minister, Sir Winston Churchill, was carrying heavy responsibility, in March 1943, his reference to children was a different one: "There is no finer investment for any community than putting milk into babies." "Or five-year-olds" he might have added. "Milk? What's that?" I can hear the climbing boys ask.

Valentine Gray has already been mentioned: he was one of many who were "obtained" from the workhouses. Inmates of workhouses were for the most part tucked away from the rest of the community; and so were the graves of a high proportion of them. John Bate and Thomas Coles and their indentures have also been mentioned. Here are some facts about some others whose lives are on record.

In 1794 John Brewster was suffocated in a flue in Stradishall, Suffolk.

In 1795 a baby of three and a half years was articled in a public house to a master-sweep.

In 1801 it was reported in the *County Herald* that the cry of someone in distress led two passers-by to enter a house. They found a boy hanging by one wrist from a beam, the other wrist tied to one of his feet; he showed signs of having been flogged. The Superintendent of the Watch was summoned and the boy was "conveyed to the humane care of the Master of Newington workhouse". The master sweep was traced and sent to trial; he was put in a pillory and given six months' imprisonment.

In 1808 a boy died of exposure on a bitterly cold February day; he had started work at three in the morning. In the same year a boy got stuck in a chimney in Walthamstow; the house-owner obtained assistance and extricated him from above, having removed several rows of bricks. The master-sweep returned to the house, struck the boy, then sent him with a bag of soot to clear another chimney, although he was weak with hunger and fatigue.

In January 1811 a boy in Wakefield fell down a flue on fire; "his flesh being completely burnt from his toes to his chin. In that state he survived the excruciating agony for five days." Also in 1811 the death of a boy was reported in the Annual Register: he came out of a chimney in Orchard Street, Westminster, and by mistake tried to return by one which had a fire at the bottom; he got stuck fast and was suffocated to death.

In 1812 Charles Barker was charged with enticing away two boys, William Bellamy and Charles Hinchcliffe, and selling them to Rose, a chimney-sweep at Kingston; the boys' age: nine years; their price: seven shillings each.

In the *Irish Farmers' Journal,* June 1813, a correspondent from County Westmeath wrote of a boy who had been sold by his mother to a sweep for three years; she had received a guinea. He reported on a County Tipperary boy who had been forced up a chimney too narrow for his body so that a wall had to be pulled down to extricate him; servants complained about so much trouble taken "about a bit of a sweep".

In 1813 a sweep named Griggs sent his boy, Thomas Pitt, about eight years old, down a brewery chimney in Upper Thames Street. The flue was "of the narrowest" and the fire barely extinguished. When the boy did not return a hole was made into the flue to pull him out – but too late, he was dead.

In 1814 George and Elizabeth Clarke of Cottingham, Yorkshire, bought a boy of about eight years old from a tinker and treated him with continual cruelty. For instance, they hung him from his wrists in a stable, and tied his leg to a horse's leg. The sweep was charged with cruelty and the Beverley Court sent him to prison and hard labour.

In 1816 a boy was forced up a chimney but could not get down. He was pulled down by the master-sweep, who dashed him on the hearth, breaking a leg; the boy died, and the sweep and his wife were charged with murder.

In 1816 the *Liverpool Mercury* reported that a boy was taken out of a flue, apparently dead; various attempts to revive him were made but without success until "two or three smart (electrical) shocks were applied to the breast", and the boy recovered.

The death of a climbing boy was reported at length in *Bell's Weekly Messenger* of 12 May 1816, under the heading: CRUELTY TO A SWEEP BOY. John Hewley, a boy of six years old, was the subject of an inquest held at the London Hospital. A witness gave evidence of extreme cruelty suffered by the boy, who was lame and could not mount the chimney; the sweep and his wife told this witness that the boy was their apprentice and that they had a right to do as they pleased with him. A student at the hospital reported on a severe blow on the head and an extensive mortification of one leg and foot.

Reports of deaths in chimneys in Scotland are rare, but the *Aberdeen Chronicle* of August 1817 gave over two columns to a report of the High Court of Justiciary at Edinburgh. The details concerning a boy stuck in a flue so horrified the reporter that he said: "the particulars are too shocking for us to repeat". One wonders what these could have been, as he did report the following: that an apprentice witnessing to the apprenticeship of the dead boy, John Fraser, aged about eleven, said that Joseph Rae the master-sweep had been known to strip the boy, tie him, gag him, flog him till he bled, then put salt brine into the wounds. It was further reported that the boy, having been stripped naked and beaten, had been forced up and down a chimney for hours for no purpose. Another apprentice reported that John Fraser had often been kept hours in a vent, on one occasion from 7 p.m. to near 3 a.m. The occasion that was being reported, because of the boy's death, showed in great detail that John Fraser had stuck so fast in a chimney that he could not extricate himself. His master had tied a rope to his leg to pull him out, and used so much force, a crowbar serving as lever, that the rope broke and the boy remained immovably fixed.

Three doctors reporting on the dead boy to the court said his death was caused either by severe pressure on the neck and spinal marrow, or by suffocation caused by his clothes getting wound round his head, or by strangulation. The Lord Justice made an impressive speech in his verdict. Joseph Rae was convicted of "culpable homicide" (not murder) and was sentenced to fourteen years' transportation. A second master-sweep, Reid, had "lent" the boy to Rae and was to be tried the following month for his participation.

In 1817 Parliament was to learn some of the answers to the question: "Who were the boys?" In that year evidence was brought before a Parliamentary Commission set up to inquire about the working of the 1788 Act. Such evidence, together with evidence at subsequent inquiries set up by Parliament (1818, 1840, 1860), bears a pathetic resemblance to the examples from other sources quoted already in this chapter. The Committee received and published reports consisting of evidence from master-sweeps themselves and from ex-climbing boys, from doctors and from men of influence who were known to have made careful investigations before giving their reports. The same subjects crop up: reports of the enticement of boys, of the sale and hiring out of boys, of floggings and other physical brutality by some masters, of the inevitable cruelty of the work, of the evasion of the law and of the efficiency of machines properly used, of the narrowness of flues and decay of chimneys, of the extreme youth of some boys (and girls) and of "sleeping black" under soot-bags; the list could go on. The Commission of 1819 heard of two girls, daughters of Morgan, who swept the chimneys at Windsor Castle, who worked for their father. There were other girls at Uxbridge, Brighton, Whitechapel, Headley in Hertfordshire, Witham in Essex, and elsewhere.

In January 1818 an eight-year-old boy of Sheffield was forced up a chimney at a very early hour, having walked four miles without food. He could not move in the chimney, which was broken just in time to save his life.

The *Irish Farmers' Journal*, ever watchful for reports about climbing boys, referred to a leaflet by S. Porter of Wallbrook, entitled: *An Appeal to the Humanity of the British Public*. This quoted statements about deaths, burns and suffocation of six boys in 1816 and eight in 1818. One report was about a child of five years old, another about a boy who was "dug out – quite dead" from an Edinburgh flue: "the most barbarous means were used to drag him down". This journal reported in March 1819 that the Bill to do away with the employment of climbing boys had been lost; the editor in spite of his humanity would not have recommended total abolition of climbing because he was of the opinion that some chimneys were impossible to clean by machines.

A climbing boy got wedged in the flue of a baker's oven in a building next to the Bank of England, where building alterations were affecting the baker's chimney. A second boy was sent down the chimney to try and release him but both became jammed and died of suffocation.

On 17 May 1818 *Bell's Weekly Messenger* reported on a boy named William Bluman. His master was summoned to appear before the Hatton Garden magistrate for having hired out his apprentice. The indenture of 1814 showed the boy to be at that time eight years of age – but in 1818 he was certainly not yet ten. He was so weak that he could hardly stand in court. The court doctor examined him and said his highly inflamed ankles and knees needed washing, poulticing, and rest, to restore them to a fit state. The boy was intimidated by his master to speak well of him, but admitted to the magistrate that the day before he had worked from 4 a.m. and had swept twenty-four flues. He wore little clothing and no cap badge to show apprenticeship. Mr Tooke, attending on behalf of the Society for Superseding the Employment of Climbing Boys, recommended that the boy's indenture be investigated as to its authenticity, and agreed to take the boy to the Holborn workhouse for care and nursing. The court doctor agreed to visit him there and report back to the magistrate.

In the *Morning Post* of Saturday 4 December 1824 is a letter, signed "X Y Z", setting out the sufferings of climbing boys and the defiance of the law by chimney-sweepers. After stating that few boys were obtained for the work without being *purchased, given away* by parish officers, or *stolen* (italics in the newspaper) the writer instanced eleven cases of extreme cruelty and death, including the two boys who died in the Lothbury baker's flue. The Coroner's

The death of two climbing boys in the flue of a chimney.
Frontispiece to *England's Climbing Boys* by Dr George Phillips.

Inquest, reported X Y Z, returned the verdict: "Accidental death." The *Morning Post* inserted further reports in their issues of 7 and 10 December 1824 and gave good publicity to James Montgomery's *Chimney-Sweeper's Friend and Climbing Boy's Album* as well as a long account of the sufferings of the boys, of the efficiency of sweeping machines, and of the obstinacy of master-sweepers.

Mary Taylor, as reported in the Sheffield *Iris* (April 1826) sold her six-year-old son to a chimney-sweep, then regretted it when she saw the open sores caused by his climbs. The parish authorities said that the trade could not be learned without this physical ordeal – and did not release him.

The *Oxford University and City Herald*, dated 14 July 1827, quoting from the *Leeds Mercury*, gave a report of a boy who died while attempting to sweep the chimney of Joseph Knowles, woolcomber. The newspaper account is as follows:

> The deceased was employed to sweep the chimney of Joseph Knowles, of Thornton, woolcomber, about 10 o'clock in the forenoon of Tuesday se'ennight, and went up very cheerfully, but from some cause or other (he himself alleged from having lost his brush) he durst not come down. Finding this, Holgate twice sent up another boy, whom he told he would be down soon enough, and then got up higher, to prevent the boy taking hold of him. He was not fast, but merely stupid. This so enraged Holgate, that he swore he would cut him in pieces, and that, when he came down, he would "give him his dinner"; he also used several other similar expressions.
>
> Holgate then lighted a fire, to bring him down, which had not the desired effect, and he at length sent up another boy, with a rope, which he fastened to the leg of the deceased, and with which Holgate pulled him down about two yards, and then fastened the rope to the bars of the grate, to prevent his ascending again. Shortly after this, Holgate went up to the deceased himself, and staid with him about five minutes, and when he came down he said he had nipped him, and felt his feet, and thought he was dying. He then shortly after went up again, and untied the rope, and on his return said he was dead

enough. The chimney was then pulled down, and the deceased taken out quite dead. That part of the chimney in which he was found was only one foot by ten inches.

When taken out it was three o'clock in the afternoon. The body, chest, and head of the deceased were opened by Dr Outhwaite, and Messrs Sharp and Trotter, of Bradford, surgeons, who found considerable fullness of blood in the vessels of the head, in all probability arising from suffocation; and on the head and body of the deceased several bruises, but none of which bruises were, in the opinion of the medical gentlemen, quite sufficient to cause death. The jury returned a verdict of manslaughter against Holgate, and he was committed, on the Coroner's warrant, to York Castle.

A reported headed POLICE appeared in *The News* on 28 September 1828. Many sweeps attended a court case where a master-sweep was summoned on a charge of assaulting one of his apprentices. The boy had been "walloped" till blood issued from his ears. The sweep explained that the boy had assaulted a smaller boy so he wrung his ears to punish him. After long questioning the magistrate said that the sweep had exceeded moderation and censured him.

In a brochure published by the Society for Superseding the Employment of Climbing Boys in 1829, examples were given of thirty boys who had suffered severely or had died in the course of their work. John Anderson, nine years old, was forced to climb a flue which was so hot that he fainted in it and died; his "master" was a woman, Ann Wilson. The apprentice of T. Young could not extricate himself from the flue which he was climbing, so Young lit straw and powder beneath him, and eventually pulled the boy down the flue by a rope tied to a leg. He was dead. The apprentice of George Fountain was lifted from the ground by his ears and flung down violently. A parish officer examining a hovel where two climbing boys slept – their total bedding consisting of soot-cloths and soot-bags – asked the sweep why pigs were allowed to be in the same small place. The answer was simple: the pigs were ill and might have died of cold elsewhere.

James Dodd's application for apprenticeship when he was eight was reported in *The Times* of 1829 and was repeated in

1929 as a subject of historical interest.

In 1830 a sweep was charged with maltreating a boy of eleven years of age; but the apprentice was found to be a girl who had worked for the man for four years.

In 1831 *The Times* reported that John Pavey, aged ten, climbed the flue of a high stack of chimneys in the Minories, London. The brickwork was decayed and gave way, causing him to fall on the parapet below, breaking his skull. The boy died. Robert Steven, the vigilant secretary of the London Society for Superseding the Employment of Climbing Boys, sent a fierce letter to *The Times* (24 January) about this boy's death. He stated that at the inquest a verdict of accidental death was brought in, and he added: "which verdict could not be otherwise so long as the law permits the barbarous custom of using children instead of brushes. . . ."

In 1832 *The Times* of 19 July reported that a six-year-old boy, a parish apprentice, was sent up a soot-filled chimney by his master, Brown of Fox Court, Gray's Inn Road. The chimney pot being crammed with soot, the boy tried to force it out, but "while enveloped in the pot" it gave way and the boy was hurled to the ground three storeys below and was seriously injured. He was taken to St Bartholomew's Hospital without hope of recovery.

In an anonymous pamphlet of 1836 it was reported that a ten-year-old boy was ordered to climb a flue at the Talbot Inn, Gloucester. As he did not descend, the master-sweep sent another of his apprentices up the flue to tie a cord round one of his legs and pull him down. This failed and the master lit brimstone matches in the flue and ordered buckets of water to be poured down from above. Next a pole was pushed down, injuring the boy's neck. After twelve hours the boy was pulled out through a hole made by a mason.

In *London Labour and the London Poor* Henry Mayhew reported that at an earlier date a sweep's boy went to the Serpentine to wash – as many London boys did – but was drowned. His fate discouraged many sweeps' boys from washing.

In 1840 Lord Shaftesbury came across a boy of four and a half years who was working for a sweep.

In 1847 Thomas Price, aged seven, was forced up a hot chimney of a chemical works in Manchester and screamed with pain. His master said: "The young devil is foxing," but the boy, having been pulled out of the flue, lost consciousness and died of convulsions within an hour. His master, John Gordon, was tried for manslaughter and sentenced to ten years' transportation.

In 1850 Samuel Whitt, a ten-year-old boy, was jammed in a hot chimney in Nottingham and died, badly burnt. There was no inquest and no one was punished. In the same year a Manchester boy of eleven died of suffocation in a heated flue.

In the *Climbing Boys' Advocate* of 1 October 1856, several reports were given, including the following. In 1848 a boy was stolen from Nottingham and sold to a chimney-sweeper at Hull. A boy of ten years of age was sold to five different sweeps at five different times and was eventually brought before the magistrates by a Mrs Chapman. He could not walk and a surgeon examined him in court. The magistrates were shocked at his appearance when the surgeon removed his bandages, and still more shocked when they learned that this enfeebled boy had been carried by his master from place to place and made to climb twelve chimneys on the previous Saturday. The Mayor called out: "Talk about slavery: there is no slavery in the world like that."

The *Advocate* reported about another lad who had been sold by his mother and was constantly maltreated by his master. On one occasion when he dropped one of his ill-fitting shoes in a ditch his angry master took him up by the leg and foot and flung him on the ground.

The Editor of the *Advocate* quoted the report of a medical officer of the Nottingham Union. The subject was James Hart, a very small boy between five and six years of age. He "was in a deplorable state. He had ulcers on his elbows, both his knees, back, fingers, toes, instep, and other parts of his body; swellings at the back of his head, ulcers arising from burns, which appeared to have been produced by putting him up a chimney. He had also scratches on his back, and contusions on his head, produced by blows. If I had not known he had been a sweep's boy, I should have thought he must have been pushed up the chimney to murder him . . .". The Editor then quoted the boy's mother: "He came home every Sunday for the first month. . . . The boy told me the defendant had made a fire at his own home and put him up the chimney and burnt his feet. He told me his master had put him in a puncheon of water, and would drown him if he did not do as he ought to do. . . ."

The Editor of the *Advocate* questioned the lot of the climbing boy:

> In order to accomplish his purpose, he must, as the case requires, toe and heel, cape and corner, recede, advance, and try again and again; and not unfrequently, in a state of nudity, have to cope with difficulties by turning and twisting in rough and angular flues, and, to add to the horror of his condition, immured in soot – contending against suffocation and death. . . . And will the community prove indifferent? Is the climbing boy to toil with unwonted exertion, and expose his life for the public good, and the community render him no assistance? The thing is impossible.

The readers learned what could be done: a resident of Exeter met a climbing boy in the street at Topsham and explained to him that he need not climb unless he pleased; he was delighted and left his master. In Birmingham sixty machines had just been supplied gratuitously to the chimney sweepers. The Inspector for the Society for Superseding the Employment of Climbing Boys had recently summoned two master-sweeps to court for employing boys and they were fined. Sweeping-machines were used in Dublin and other Irish towns: "the late Admiral Oliver extensively aided the cause in that country".

Jackson's *Oxford Journal* for 13 May 1865 reported a Petty Sessions case in which a sweep was discharged. He had been brought before the court charged with allowing his apprentice to climb a chimney. The reason for his discharge was that he was not "with the boy at the time" – thus was the law mocked, for how could the master accompany his apprentice?

In the 1870s Lord Shaftesbury and others had their attention drawn to the death of a ten-year-old Leeds boy by suffocation in a flue; and to similar deaths of a Durham boy and of a Staffordshire boy. In 1872 Christopher Drummond died at the age of seven-and-a-half; he met his death climbing the flue of a fernery at Washington Hall, Gateshead.

And at last George Brewster in 1875: an eleven-year-old

boy who could not know that he was to earn the title of the last boy to die as a result of climbing a chimney. *The Times* reported the Assize Court trial of Brewster's master, William Wyer, on 24 March 1875, and on 25 March gave a column and a half of editorial comment in a leading article. The *Cambridge Chronicle* of 27 March gave a full report, and other papers publicized the death of the boy and the trial of his master.

One of the comments in *The Times* article was that at the Fulbourn Hospital where the boy died there was:

> one of those scenes of fatal, deliberate and inexcusable cruelty which for more than half a century have been among the worst and the most obstinate, though still the most universally recognized, public scandals of this Kingdom.

Lord Shaftesbury once again presented a Bill to Parliament: this was passed. The Act was enforceable and so no more boys climbed flues.

The circumstances of George Brewster's story are these. His parents lived in London. His mother became ill and his married brother, William, adopted him and subsequently passed him to another married brother, John, who allowed him to be apprenticed to William Wyer. A third brother, Bernard, testified in Court that George was eleven years ten months old: according to the sweep he was fourteen. Wyer had the contract to sweep the flues of three boilers at Fulbourn Hospital, Cambridge, three times a year. In court the stoker reported the method of cleaning the flues and stated that on this occasion George took off his coat, put on a cap covering his face, and went into a flue of which the door was twelve inches by six. In about a quarter of an hour the boy was pulled out by Wyer in an exhausted state. A doctor was summoned. He found the boy alive and he removed "soot and stuff" from his mouth. The doctor gave him brandy and put him in a warm bath, but he died in a short time. A *post mortem* examination revealed that the arms were abraded, the head congested, and there was much black powder in the lungs and windpipe. The cause of death was given as suffocation.

An architect was called as a witness. He showed plans of the flues and boilers and revealed that the flue in question was over eleven feet long. A detective sergeant reported that he had served Wyer with a notice eleven years earlier for contravening "Lord Shaftesbury's Acts". Some local people of influence testified to Wyer's normally kind conduct towards his apprentice.

The jury took one minute to find the sweep guilty. The Judge sentenced Wyer to six months' hard labour. He spoke forcibly about the infraction of an Act which had been passed for humane purposes, and asked that other chimney-sweeps be informed about this case. He added that if in future similar cases came before him the sentence would be more severe.

Of course, some boys gave up climbing. Having grown up in the underworld of a city they were able to drift into the world of crime. One boy landed in Newgate Prison whence, thanks to his early skill in climbing, he escaped, climbing virtually unclimbable walls and negotiating un-negotiable *chevaux-de-frise* surrounding the prison.

As we shall see in the chapters on The Campaigners, some boys were befriended: Lord Shaftesbury and Robert Steven went to great trouble to rescue a boy from his apprenticeship: arrangements for him to be brought up and educated were made. He was, according to Lord Shaftesbury's diary of 19 September 1840, "gentle, and of a sweet disposition; we all know he has suffered . . .". A boy was befriended by Joseph Johnson, printer, another by Robert Southey, poet. There are stories of boys being kidnapped and being found by their parents. A well-to-do couple in Yorkshire became interested in a boy who fell down one of their chimneys; they recognized him as a boy of gentle birth but could not trace his family. They arranged for his upbringing. Parson Woodforde recorded in his diary that his sweep Holland had a new boy who nearly lost his life by getting stuck in one of the parsonage chimneys; the Parson gave him sixpence, and perhaps his kindness went further than that.

The mortality rate of all children in the period of this book was high compared with today's rate. The mortality rate of climbing boys was very high indeed. What chances had boys who were "stunted in growth, blear-eyed from soot, knapped-kneed from climbing when the bones were soft" of becoming grown men?

Yet some climbing boys did survive and live to old age. One, Joseph Lawrence, swept flues continuously from his apprenticeship in 1755 till his retirement as master-sweep in 1816. History records him as a humane master who taught his assistants to read and write and insisted on a weekly scrubbing so that they could attend church service in a reasonably clean state. Another boy of the same name was apprenticed at the age of twelve in 1857 to a sweep named William Specie, of Henley. It was already illegal under the 1840 Act for a boy under twenty-one to climb flues, and under sixteen to assist master-sweeps. However, Joseph completed his apprenticeship, took up other work, and died at the age of 104 in 1949 in Surrey.

Peter Hall, born in 1804 at Stockport, had been a climbing boy at the age of six and a half. At fifty-eight he acted as agent for the North Staffordshire and Birmingham Society for Superseding the Employment of Climbing Boys. He travelled round the country and in 1862 gave evidence on the violation of the law concerning climbing boys. As he had himself taken master-sweeps to court and had obtained four hundred convictions he was justified in his claim that violation of the law was on the increase. He reported also that there were more violations in those towns where Societies for Superseding were not active.

History records too that William Harris died as an old man in 1920 at Leighton Buzzard, having been one of the last of the climbing boys; and that Daniel Dye lived till 1940 – he was then ninety-three years of age and had been a climbing boy some eighty years earlier.

Perhaps Edward Montagu deserves mention: he had what was described as "a variegated career". He ran away three times from Westminster School, and on one occasion, according to the Annual Register of 1776, he exchanged clothes with a sweep and followed that occupation for a time. If he did in fact climb chimneys he must have been one of the few boys to have voluntarily chosen that career.

There exist many photos of splendid old sweeps wearing their top-hats with great dignity: if they had been climbing boys they must have been either very tough or lucky enough to have worked for humane masters.

A boy named James Seaward deserves recognition in this chapter. Born in 1863 at Wokingham, Berkshire, he started climbing chimneys at an early age and there is no record that he came to any harm. There is a strong tradition that it was he who climbed the chimneys of Charles Kingsley's Rectory at Eversley, Hampshire, and that he was the model for Tom in *The Water Babies*. He was elected to the Town Council of Wokingham in 1892 and became an alderman, a position he held until shortly before his death in 1921. He was a member of the Baptist Church and having voluntarily taken on the annual cleaning of the flues of his church he continued to do so for over fifty years – a generous gesture for which he was publicly thanked.

And so, who were the boys? Only a small proportion of them have been singled out for mention in this chapter. Most climbing boys were ignored by the majority of the population of their day, but just a few were brought out of their black backgrounds by the humanitarians who campaigned for them for a hundred and two years.

CHAPTER 3
The Early Campaigners

We are constantly reminded of the hard battle that always has to be fought, whenever the dictates of humanity come into conflict with motives of self-interest.
EDWIN HODDER, *Life and Work of the 7th Earl of Shaftesbury* (1886)

Now I have introduced a number of boys – named and unnamed – to represent the hundreds and thousands who swarmed up and down chimneys in the hundred and two years ending in 1875. If the introductions have been painful may I add that I have omitted many descriptions which were too distressing to repeat: descriptions for the most part given at the Parliamentary inquiries of 1818 and 1840.

How did the boys' plight first come to light? How and when did it come to an end?

The importance of Jonas Hanway (1712–86) in the campaign against the boys' climbing conditions cannot be overestimated. It was he who provided the basis on which the campaign started, and he created publicity which others were to develop. As a young man he travelled far. In the part of China which he visited he learned that no questions were asked of parents who killed a new-born baby. He thought his own compatriots were kinder than that, and on returning to England he investigated conditions in work-houses in 1765. He was horrified to find that in one London workhouse 64 out of 78 children admitted in a year had died; in another, 16 out of 18 died, in another not one child survived in fourteen years. He published his findings. A committee was set up by the House of Commons to check his figures, for Parliament was sensible of its responsibility for workhouses.

Members of the Committee found to their dismay that out of 100 children admitted to orphanages, only 7 survived. Hoping to improve conditions, Parliament passed an Act: it was ruled that children must be boarded out and kept no longer than three weeks in workhouses. On inquiring ten years later if the Act was being enforced, Parliament learned that the mortality rate for "parish infants" had fallen

considerably. But baby-farming began to flourish.

Hanway made friends with a certain master-sweep, David Porter, and together they formulated, as early as 1770, several ideas for regulating the work of the boys. They recommended that a fraternity provide a proper apprentice-ship. If their ideas had been carried through, the story of the climbing boys in the nineteenth century would not have been the long drawn-out story that we find it to be.

Jonas Hanway, now an experienced investigator, carried out research into the conditions of sweeps' apprentices. He found that no one except master-sweeps required the under-sized children from the Poor Law for apprentices: chimney flues were small and were to become smaller. Sweeps' handbills would emphasize this; "small boys for small flues" was often printed in the advertisement. Master-sweeps and guardians of workhouses tried to show that by apprenticing boys to the sweeps' trade they were benefiting the master-sweeps, the ratepayers, and the boys themselves.

Hanway called meetings, advised on indenture forms, consulted master-sweeps, talked to boys. He described one of the boys he met: shaped like the letter S because of his work, the boy was blind as well as deformed and stunted. From the point of view of the job, his shape was an advantage to him in climbing up and down. His blindness was of no significance to his master.

The nature of the work shocked Hanway, and so did the indentures. He asserted that, at a time when humanitarians were calling out for the abolition of slavery in the New World, climbing boys themselves were slaves. A boy could be bound without any say in the matter, and under much pressure, to a master, callous or otherwise. When finally a boy left the master's control, he had no skill except for climbing chimneys.

In 1773 Hanway published *The State of Chimney Sweepers' Young Apprentices,* and in 1774 and again in 1780 he helped to form associations aimed at improving conditions.

Responsible apprenticeship was in the forefront of Hanway's mind when, having formed a committee in 1773 on behalf of sweeps' apprentices, he sent out letters to all master-sweeps of London; he enclosed revised indenture forms but found few master-sweeps were sympathetic to his ideas. Lord Shaftesbury was to refer to the letters of "good Jonas Hanway" a hundred and two years later.

Hanway had become a prolific journalist. He sent out further letters in the form of a series to the *Public Advertiser,* describing the neglect of common humanity towards the boys. These letters, eighteen in number, he collected together and published as a book entitled *Sentimental History of Chimney Sweeps in London and Westminster* (1785). He elaborated the title with the words: "Showing the Necessity of Putting them under Regulations to prevent the grossest inhumanity to the Climbing Boys etc." and subtitled it: "A

The abject child of Misery's sad train
Still looks on one below

Frontispiece to *Sentimental History of Chimney Sweeps in London and Westminster* by Jonas Hanway.

Petition to Humanity". Hanway stressed this appeal to humanity: and the frontispiece of his book is the picture of two ragged dirty climbing boys, one on crutches, with St Paul's Cathedral forming a significant background. The two boys acted as representatives of the four hundred climbing boys who, Hanway estimated, were apprenticed in 1785 to one hundred master-sweeps in London and Westminster.

The *Sentimental History* was beautifully bound and excellently printed. The letters were open letters to such people as the Lord Mayor of London and the Magistrates of London and Westminster; one letter is to London clergymen on the subject of the provision of Sunday Schools. In addition were copies of those letters which had already been sent to master-sweeps recommending regulations for their trade.

Hanway's interests were wide and his Christianity was practical. His desire for justice was extended to all classes. He expressed strong disapproval of those churches where the beadle on duty evicted sweeps' boys.

From 1760 onwards Jonas Hanway had been gaining sympathizers: "but," he said sadly, "we had not then skill or perseverance enough to succeed." He referred to "Ambulator" who had written to the *Public Advertiser* in 1760 about the number of barefoot boys, demanding that the masters should be summoned before the magistrate to enforce proper clothing.

Hanway's letters managed to impress a number of humane magistrates. This is not surprising, for the information he had collected was startling. Hanway found out for himself the size of the chimney flues and published the measurements and pointed out that it was an offence to humanity to employ boys for such chimneys. Edinburgh, he stated, had solved the problem by putting the sweeping of chimneys under the control of police. Boys were not employed there as assistants, and the sweeps themselves cleaned the chimneys by the relatively simple method of lowering and raising bundles of twigs on sticks. Hanway was not to know that in 1817 an Edinburgh sweep, Joseph Rae, was to be found guilty of the culpable homicide of his apprentice: police control in that city was not complete. Hanway was not to know, either, that no chimney-sweepers' act was to be effective until 1875, when the English police would be empowered to carry out the law.

Hanway made practical suggestions in his letters. He urged that boys should no longer be forced up chimneys that were actually on fire, and that they should be adequately fed, washed and lodged. He said also that they should receive education. Hanway was a whole century before his time! What did that Victorian housewife say when she heard that her sweep's climbing boy was to receive education? "Education? What next?"

Hanway's book contains a picture of a clean and upright German sweep with ladder and all–over protective clothing; it is a reminder that chimneys on the Continent were not in general climbed on the inside.

Hanway wanted above all that the readers of his book should consider the principles – moral, religious and political – on which boys should be apprenticed; he pointed out the hardships and unjust treatment which the boys were enduring at the time. He felt strongly that Christianity should be brought into the boys' lives. He advocated organizations to administer Sunday Schools for them and he

A German Chimney Sweeper.

Erect in posture, in strength confirmed,
His smutty Task performed he smiles unhurt.

thought that the officers of these would supervise the activities of the apprentices as controlled by their masters. It was because of Jonas Hanway's influence that religion was mentioned in the 1788 Act.

Universal education was not on the statute book till 1870; involvement of educationalists with the social welfare of the pupils did not make itself apparent till the twentieth century. Jonas Hanway, in befriending the boys and concerning himself with their religious and educational upbringing, was looking far into the future.

Hanway reported in his book that orphans in vagabond state, and the bastards of the poorest people, were sold to sweeps, and he condemned their bad clothes, bad sleeping arrangements, lack of washing facilities, and the fact that they could not achieve "proper discharge by perspiration". He reported with unfeigned horror that "young females" were employed to go up chimneys. Shortly before his death in 1786 he sent an eloquent letter to the Lords Commissioners of the Treasury pressing the claim of the unprotected apprentices.

Hanway had started something: something which was to move in jerks for a century. He died before he saw any results, but his contemporaries and successors saw that his recommendations for better conditions were brought before Parliament. A Commission of Inquiry was set up in 1788, to investigate the sweeps' profession; and the appalling cruelty and neglect of the climbing boys was revealed in the Commission's report.

Mr Robert Burton introduced a Bill in Parliament in the same year and this was passed. Henceforth no boy should be bound before he was eight years old – but who could check a boy's age? His parents' consent must be obtained, and the master-sweep must promise to provide suitable clothing and living conditions, as well as an opportunity to attend church on Sundays. Hanway had wanted master-sweeps to be compelled to take out a licence, and a clause to this effect was inserted in the Bill. However, although the Bill was passed, this clause was thrown out by the Lords – and this was not the only time that the Lords were to throw out something which would have been to the advantage of climbing boys. The clause being rejected, the Act proved to be practically unenforceable.

The Bill, however, had become an Act, and the passing of the Act may be said to have started the real campaign to help the boys. In the same year, 1788, David Porter, Hanway's friend, sent a petition to Parliament about climbing boys' conditions and in 1792 he published *Considerations of the Present State of Chimney Sweepers with some Observations on the Act of Parliament intended for their Regulation and Relief. . . .* This pamphlet opens with a study of the last twenty years of chimney-sweeping and pays tribute to two men, Hanway and Thornton, for being among the first to campaign for better conditions of employment. At this time Porter estimated that the number of boys apprenticed to master-sweeps had risen to five hundred.

A humane master-sweep himself, David Porter attempted through his writing to carry the campaign further than the 1788 Act. To promote better conditions of employment he asked that sweeps' boys should have a change of clothing, should have facilities for washing clean, should have one good dinner a week, should be protected from catching sweeps' cancer, and should be taught to read and write: these seem to be modest requirements if related to twentieth-century standards.

David Porter suffered from the frustration common to other campaigners, and spoke sadly of using his talents to achieve unmerited misery for himself. He instanced reasons for his frustration: the Sweeps' Friendly Society founded in 1770 lasted only a few months; the 1788 Bill had been reduced in authority and value by the House of Lords and was difficult to enforce; the apprenticeship cap badge was of little use, especially if the master-sweep was moving from place to place. Sweeps – and there were too many of them anyway – were easily led to fraud; the sale of soot to farmers was often the subject of fraud and needed regulating.

David Porter distributed an elaborate trade leaflet to advertise his own trade. It refers proudly to the Princess Amelia as a client, and is illustrated by a reproduction of the royal coat of arms and a picture of himself in elegant clothes, speaking to a client, his four climbing boys standing by to await his orders. His guarantee to cure "smoking chimneys" is followed by the remark: No Cure No Pay.

David Porter emphasized that his only object was to help

his fellow-tradesmen. It is surprising therefore that he was later on to modify his aim; this showed itself when he gave evidence to the House of Lords Committee in 1818. By this time Porter was a prosperous builder and land-owner. His evidence indicated that boys were more efficient than machines – evidence which some of the Lords wanted to hear.

However, Porter's writing proved of value to the campaign. In 1796 a society was formed: "for Bettering the Condition and Increasing the Comforts of the Poor", and a vigorous member of this was Sir Thomas Bernard. He read Porter's book with appreciation and asked that copies be supplied to fellow-members of his society. One of them, the Bishop of Durham, was personally concerned in founding a Sunday School at Kingston, Surrey in 1798; this was for climbing boys, and an unnamed Lady Bountiful gave clothes and bedding to the boys: clothes and bedding such as they had never possessed before.

This Society, which aimed to better the conditions of the poor, was one of many which were coming into being from the end of the eighteenth century onwards: humanitarianism was stirring in the aftermath of the Industrial Revolution. George III gave his patronage to the 1796 Society, a matter of some significance.

The members of the Society tried among other things to rouse public opinion over the treatment of climbing boys, and Jonas Hanway's book of 1785 and David Porter's book of 1792 proved of great value to them. Out of their Society grew the London Society for Superseding the Necessity for Employing Climbing Boys.

This London Society was founded in 1803 by William Tooke, an artist and a humanitarian. The Bishop of Durham became President, and influential vice-presidents were elected. One of these was William Wilberforce, already celebrated for his struggle to get black slavery abolished. He became deeply concerned for "the little black slaves" of our own land.

The Society attracted some of the more responsible master-sweeps, and they helped to provide information about the employment and living conditions of the boys. The Society asked for information about the sizes of flues and learnt that seven-inch by seven-inch flues were known to have been climbed by children, information which they were able to give later to a Select Committee of Parliament.

The knowledge was beginning to circulate that the climbers were "human brushes". How to "supersede" them? The Society took the practical step of promoting a competition for mechanical brushes. A certain George Smart thought one evening how a strong and flexible rod could be made, made it up the same night and swept all the chimneys of his house with it before the servants were up. A few days later he entered for the Society's prize of a medal and was awarded it; the Society then publicized the brush. As George Smart explained later to Dr Lushington, his long flexible rod was made on the same principle as the rods made by children who thread string through tobacco-pipes.

The following year George Smart won a prize of £50 for promoting the use of the machine to "supersede" the employment of boys; and money prizes for sweeping one hundred and three hundred chimneys without using boys were awarded to Richard Paige of Guilford Street, London, and to James Laver, of Walthamstow. As the years went on, more and more sweeping-machines were used, but still boys – who were cheaper – continued to be used.

Publicity about the machine reached Ireland and from the early part of the century the *Irish Farmers' Journal* reported on this, and gave its strong support to the campaign to ameliorate the lot of the climbing boys.

Other Societies for Superseding the Employment of Climbing Boys came into being. The Sheffield Society was founded in 1807 and was convinced:

> that the practice ought not to be tolerated at all in a Christian country; and that if the cruelty which is unavoidable in seasoning tender infants for this most repulsive of occupations, were inflicted on brute animals the legislation would promptly forbid it.

This is strong language. The words "a Christian country" and "seasoning tender infants" should have touched the consciences of the readers. Already the idea that the British are more kindly towards animals than towards children was beginning to creep in.

At their May 1807 meeting, the Sheffield Committee stated that by paying attention to the conditions of the

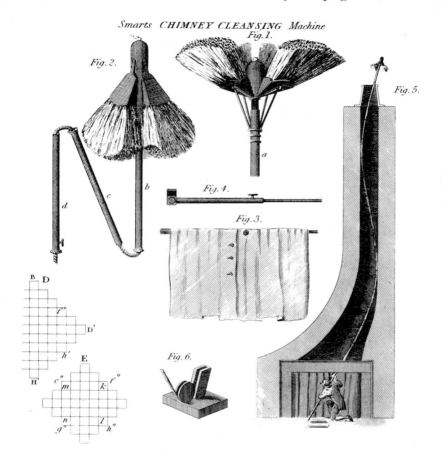

Smarts *CHIMNEY CLEANSING* Machine

Hurst, Rees, Orme & Brown, Paternoster Row, London.

Lowry sculp.

children's work, and by enforcing the Acts of Parliament concerning chimney-sweepers, the conditions of those who had to climb could be improved. The members resolved to investigate the machine-sweeping arrangements by consulting the London Society, and decided that:

> as soon as posible (they) shall engage an ingenious, active, honest Man to undertake the management of the said Machines, and to accustom himself to the use of them and that when he shall have become sufficiently expert in the use of them (*and not before*), the public shall be solicited to

employ him, and that he then shall instruct such others in the art as the demand shall seem to require.

The members had much to discuss. They resolved further to appeal for money to testify "the approbation of those who are friendly to the attempt, and for defraying the charge of purchasing Machines . . . and other expenses". The report states that a subscription fund was begun "with great liberality".

The Chairman of the meeting was Mr Sorby, Master Cutler, an influential man in the growing city of Sheffield. The meeting elected a committee and three of the members on it were Mr Sorby, Samuel Roberts, and James Montgomery: the last two will appear elsewhere in this book.

By 1816 the Society for Superseding the Employment of Climbing Boys decided that it had enough support to send a recommendation to Parliament for a new law to replace the 1788 one: this time to prohibit the use of climbing boys altogether. A number of respectable master-sweeps were valuable members of the Society for Superseding the Employment of Climbing Boys, but opposition to them was created by other master-sweeps who were afraid to lose their apprentices. When they learned of the campaign for prohibiting the use of climbing boys they organized themselves with a view to preventing such parliamentary action, and set about raising funds for their expenses. They were determined to spread the idea that machines were insufficient and tried to convince their customers by scattering soot and blocking flues when using the machines. They may have managed to raise the funds they needed, but the records of the Hand-in-Hand Insurance Society show that in 1818 the master-sweeps solicited funds in vain from that society: its secretary was the energetic Robert Steven, who had been championing climbing boys for years.

It would seem that at the time when branches of the Society for Superseding the Employment of Climbing Boys were establishing themselves, men in different parts of the country were writing articles on the subject of the boys' employment. One of these was published in 1816 anonymously "by a chimney sweeper"; it was a four-page leaflet and could be bought at 4 shillings for a hundred copies. It was illustrated by a diagram of the flues in a four-storeyed chimney stack and gave precise information about a builder who had constructed chimneys in different parts of London, and had superintended over a period of time the sweeping of 20,000 chimneys. He described the way the boy had to climb, its difficulties and dangers. He supplied some figures: in five years he knew of fifteen boys being suffocated to death, six burnt to death, one smothered in rubbish, and two killed by falling. He emphasized the hardships in winter and the periods of unemployment in summer and pointed out that boys could be discharged at sixteen with no useful skill and no resources: hence very often a turn to crime. The writer pointed out that there was no need to discharge them: they could learn to use the sweeping-machine. He mentioned the offer of a Mrs Denyer to pay £200 to the inventor of a good sweeping-machine.

Those master-sweeps who organized themselves as champions of the boys annoyed other master-sweeps who wanted to retain boys and to refuse the use of sweeping-machines. A group of such master-sweeps became very active in Bristol and in 1817 four of them published their own booklet of twenty-four pages, giving as its thesis: "there are two sides to every question". It set out to counter every statement in a pamphlet from York: this described the harsh conditions of apprentices' work, their illnesses and deaths, and the sweeping-machine which could replace them. The Bristol sweeps denied that work and living conditions of the boys were harsh, expressed ignorance of illness, stunted growth, deformity and death among their boys, and affirmed that soot cancer was unknown. The booklet provided diagrams of chimneys with explanatory details to prove that machines could not clean them.

According to the booklet, the employment compared favourably with that of other children at the time, and a cheerful feast provided by a Captain Budworth for sweeps and apprentices in 1809 was mentioned with an emphasis on the happiness, cleanliness and good health of all the guests.

The booklet did not help the campaigners against the employment of climbing boys. It was published in Bristol in the same month – June 1817 – that the Sheffield Society for Superseding the Employment of Climbing Boys was presenting a petition to Parliament to bring in a new Act. The

Sheffield Society was first: within a few days the London branch of the Society sent a similar petition. The House of Commons acted promptly by setting up a committee to inquire into the whole matter, and the Hon. Henry Grey Bennet was appointed chairman. His Committee took up their work at once and carried their responsibilities so seriously that their findings, based on authenticated reports, have provided a valuable fund of information about the climbing boys' employment. The information bore a strong resemblance to that which Jonas Hanway had reported over thirty years earlier.

Evidence about the master-sweeps' trade was called for from members of the Society for Superseding the Employment of Climbing Boys – men who had been collecting information for years; evidence was given by George Smart and other inventors of sweeping-machines; it was given by doctors who had attended boys in hospital or who had given evidence at inquests; it was given by architects and builders, and by a number of master-sweeps themselves.

Some of the information offered by master-sweeps was very valuable. For example, a master-sweep named Thomas Edmunds testified that he had used Smart's machine from 1804 and that he had swept 1313 chimneys in 1816 by machine only. John Harding, chimney-sweep for twenty-three years, used the machine without employing any assistant; he answered over a hundred questions of the Committee about the work and working conditions of the climbing boys. Another named Thomas Allen had been "articled at 4½ years" in a public house. He used nothing but Smart's machine.

There are two appendices to the report from the Committee which was set up to investigate the employment of climbing boys. One appendix concerns the master-sweeps who at a general meeting urged the improvement of working conditions, but not the abolition of the employment. The other was drawn up by a group of surveyors and builders. They recommended the abolition of the employment of the boys and urged that the chimneys be properly constructed. Such recommendations coming from practical men must have encouraged the campaigners; "proper construction" would necessitate the employment of skilled bricklayers and of men to supervise them while work was in progress. Supervision always was, and still is, difficult to ensure.

So clearly was it shown that the 1788 Act was being flouted – an insult to Parliament itself – and so horrific was the evidence of the cruelty to the apprentices, that the Committee was ready to recommend the immediate abolition of the employment of climbing boys.

In less than a month since his appointment as chairman, Mr Bennet was ready to propose an amendment of the 1788 Act, but on a technicality his proposed bill did not go through. Almost at once the Society for Superseding the Employment of Climbing Boys took action. They printed the report given by Mr Bennet and, making use of this for increasing publicity, they urged that public meetings be held in cities and towns throughout England. They said that they were acting:

> for the protection of those who, for the most part, are foundlings or orphans, who have no other guardian than the State; who have no option in the selection of their trade; who are oppressed because they are helpless; who labour because they are weak; who perform the hardest service at a period when they are least able to endure it, and with whom every principle of beneficial employment is reversed; thus constituting at once a stigma on our humanity, and a humiliating limit to the boasted fertility of our mechanical resources.

Could any committee have expressed itself more clearly?

Mr Bennet did not drop the subject. In February 1818 he proposed introducing a new bill for regulating the trade of chimney-sweeping; his proposal showed some modifications of the 1817 Bill and it received support from petitions which came in from numerous public meetings held all over the country. Opposition arose, arguments that had been put forward the year before were repeated and were again countered. A committee heard statements by the organized chimney-sweepers who were still wanting to retain boys; but the committee heard evidence too from responsible men such as surgeons, architects, fire-insurance officials and firemen, builders and others.

A surgeon, Mr Richard Wright, gave medical evidence from his experience at Guy's and St Bartholomew's

Hospitals. He spoke of the deformities caused to the young boys by the climbs up and down chimneys and by their loads of heavy bags of soot, sometimes carried great distances. He spoke also of the cancer which often attacked the scrotum and said that many victims did not apply for medical help because they dreaded the operation by the knife. Mr Wright's medical evidence covered the stunted growth of the young boys, the burns caused by chimneys on fire or overheated, the exposure to all weathers, the chest complaints, the state of starvation which encouraged them to thieve and embark on a life of crime, or the provision of unsuitable food which could lead to debility, scurvy and other illnesses. Mr Wright had evidence of mutilated limbs caused by various types of accidents in the climbs.

A remarkable speech was made by Dr Lushington, philanthropist and member of the Society for Superseding the Employment of Climbing Boys. Dr Lushington held nothing back: he spoke of the practice of kidnapping or of buying children, he spoke of violent methods used to force children up dark and evil-smelling flues, he described the sores on knees and elbows rubbed with brine or saltpetre to harden, he spoke of the accidents, the misshapen limbs, the cancer of the scrotum, the boys' constant fear of being suffocated or lost in flues. The doctor declared that machines would clean nearly every flue – and the few which could not be cleaned on account of angles could have soot-doors inserted where they were necessary.

When the Bill came to the House of Lords some members thought – in spite of all the evidence – that more harm could be caused to the community if machines alone were used than could be compensated by bettering the boys' conditions of work: they postponed the Bill.

Again in 1819 Mr Bennet asked permission of the House of Commons to introduce a bill for regulating the trade. He summarized the 1817 report. A new member, Ommaney, had been urged by master-sweeps to support them and oppose the bill; his opinions were that it would injure the public interest as the machines were not efficient enough, that the parish officials would not be able to apprentice their indigent charges to master-sweeps, and that the sins of the fathers were being visited on the boys because many of them were "children of rich men begotten in an improper manner". He added another comment of his own: that many boys were "gay, cheerful, and contented".

Against some opposition the Bill was passed in the Commons and went to the House of Lords. Lord Lauderdale ridiculed the whole subject, with the result that the Lords voted against it. There was still no enforceable legislation to support the boys' cause.

However, the limelight of Parliament had been turned on the boys. Public meetings throughout the country were making it possible for all people to know about the working conditions. On the Isle of Wight the people of Newport, on learning of the death of Valentine Gray, in January 1822, were so distressed that they decided to bring to an end the deaths of climbing boys by publicizing the circumstances of his death. They erected an imposing memorial to the boy in a Newport graveyard and had the following words incised on it:

TO THE MEMORY
OF VALENTINE GRAY
THE LITTLE SWEEP
INTERRED JANUARY THE 5th
A.D. 1822
IN THE 10th YEAR OF HIS AGE.
IN TESTIMONY OF
THE GENERAL FEELING
FOR SUFFERING INNOCENCE
THIS MONUMENT
IS ERECTED BY PUBLIC SUBSCRIPTION

Valentine Gray had other champions. The Visitors and Guardians of Alverstoke Workhouse, in reporting Valentine's death, exonerated themselves of culpability but added:

They are the first in strongly recommending to their successors that the measure of apprenticing boys from the Poorhouse to persons exercising the trade of Chimney Sweeper should be abandoned . . . as well from the difficulty of watching over their conduct and the expense of punishing them then acting contrary to law, as from a feeling towards the boys themselves who should seem to enter on that line of life solely with a view of being liberated from the restraint of a poorhouse. . . .

The medical profession knew about the boys' conditions of employment. Under the title "Chimney Sweepers' Cancer" a detailed account by Mr Henry Earle appeared in *Medico-Chirurgical Transactions* in March 1823; and in the same month a medical report on the same subject, by Mr Pott, appeared in the *Analytical Review*. He stated:

A warty excrescence . . . discharges a thin acrimonious ichor, which excoriates the surrounding skin. Ulceration now takes place in the centre, and the edges of the wound become everted, and throw out a luxuriant growth, with scirrhous hardness, which discharges a very fetid irritating matter. The most common situation for this complaint is the lower part of the scrotum . . . it not infrequently extends itself to one or both testicles. . . . The disease, in every instance that I have seen, except one, extended itself to the parts immediately contiguous. . . . The countenance has a peculiar leaden hue, and the general health is materially affected by the severity of the pain, the want of rest, and the constitution having to contend with a disease which it is incapable of throwing off. . . . The scalpel is the only resource. . . .

Then in 1824 came forward another campaigner: James Montgomery of Sheffield published a book. James Montgomery (1771–1854) had a varied career: as a radical journalist he served three years in York gaol for sedition. By 1825 he had become a moderate Conservative and received a pension from Sir Robert Peel. He wrote poems and hymns: some of his compositions are in *Hymns Ancient and Modern*. In a volume of verse called *The West Indies* he pleaded for the abolition of the slave trade. Like Hanway, and like William Wilberforce and many others, James Montgomery saw a connection between the enslavement of black people and the forced labour of soot-engrimed boys.

Indeed he was involved in so many philanthropic activities that after his death a monument "in memory of their revered townsman" was commissioned by the people of Sheffield. The work of the sculptor James Bell, it shows a bronze figure of James Montgomery, and it was unveiled on 29 July 1861. It was moved from the Sheffield General Cemetery to the Cathedral ground in 1971, where it was rededicated. James Montgomery is not forgotten.

MONTGOMERY

JAMES MONTGOMERY

He edited the *Sheffield Iris* (formerly the *Sheffield Register*) from 1794 for over thirty years; it was a paper that had a reputation for forceful and outspoken opinions even before Montgomery became editor. He was imprisoned in 1795 and 1796, first for printing a song, "The Fall of the Bastille", secondly for reporting on a riot in Sheffield. He had a missionary zeal which activated his conscience both in private life and in his editorial chair.

He conceived the idea of collecting information about sweeps' climbing boys and publishing it in a book, adding to it an Album of literary contributions all concerned with climbing boys. This entailed writing to many of his literary and academic friends and soliciting contributions.

It was this "Album" of Montgomery's which suggested to me the idea of providing a literary album to form the last chapter of this book. Montgomery's book: *The Chimney-Sweeper's Friend and Climbing Boy's Album* (1824) is rarely to be found now, but the author's autographed copy is kept at the Wellcome Institute Library in London.

Montgomery, having helped to found the Sheffield Society for Superseding the Employment of Climbing Boys (1807), produced the book on behalf of that society. It was dedicated to King George III, who was already patron of the London Society. The preface sets out the ideas which made Montgomery write the book:

> The barbarity of the practice cannot be denied – nor can it be mitigated, for it is next to impossible to teach a child this trade at all, without the infliction of such cruelties upon his person, as would subject a master to any *other* business to the discipline of Bridewell, were he to exercise the like on *his* apprentice. . . .
>
> There are *machines in use*, with which 99 chimneys out of a 100 might be swept, and the danger to the boys in ascending those which machines cannot thoroughly cleanse, namely, angular, tortuous, dilapidated, and *ignited* flues – is so imminent that when death ensues . . . the master, who puts a child to such a task, should be punished for feloniously slaying; and in few instances would it be too severe to implicate those who suffer such outrages to be committed in their dwellings as accessories before the fact.

This stern idea of implicating "accessories before the fact" was repeated in *The Times* leader a half-century later, when commenting on the death of the boy George Brewster (1875).

Montgomery continued:

> The remedy for this evil is simple, obvious, and certain – let the legislature prohibit the masters from taking any more children as climbers, and, before the present race have outgrown their detestable occupation, there will be improved machines to sweep any chimney.

Montgomery saw the remedy as "simple, obvious and certain". Other campaigners must have concurred with this. Montgomery's book, which resembled Jonas Hanway's in its presentation of facts, was published a half-century after the *Sentimental History*. The campaign was to continue for another half-century after the publication of *The Chimney-Sweeper's Friend*.

Widow selling her son to a chimney sweep.

James Montgomery's book is illustrated by Robert Cruikshank. The frontispiece gives the picture of a widow selling her small son to a sweep; he is a clean boy, while a filthy one – already apprenticed – sits on the ground, being sniffed at by a dog. In the left background of the picture is a lady with befeathered hat, shaded by a dainty parasol, and she sits in her carriage attended by a coachman and two flunkeys. In the right background of the picture is a fair-sized house, with a sweep and his brush emerging from a chimney. The picture is intended to emphasize "the haves and the have-nots" of the 1820s – the upper and lower classes.

Another picture shows a small boy on his knees begging "a noble legislator" to amend the law – his master is ascending a ladder and a couple of geese in his hand are to be used in his job. The reference to the "noble legislator" is to Lord Lauderdale, who has been mentioned already. It was his jokes in the House of Lords (1818) about geese and ducks being sent down chimneys to clean them which reduced the subject to mockery and succeeded in getting the Lords to throw out the Bill.

The picture illustrates a poem which James Montgomery printed in the Album. It is entitled "The Lay of the Last Chimney Sweeper", by R.R., and it puts the case of "the poor infant sweeps compared to ducks and geese".★

Lord Lauderdale was not forgotten. Later, after the death of a grandson in a fire, Montgomery referred to Lord Lauderdale when he remarked that he thought no member of the House of Lords would ever again joke about children being burnt to death. Lord Lauderdale was the subject of ridicule in a "comic drama" at the royal Olympic Theatre in London in 1832: his scornful speech of 1819 was not treated lightly by the campaigners.

The first part of Montgomery's book contains statements describing the work of the boys, the accidents and deaths of many of them – in fact, his book is largely a summary of the evidence given to the Parliamentary Committee of 1817, on "Employment of Boys in Sweeping of Chimnies".

★ The practice of sending geese down chimneys persisted in Eire until recently; several people wrote to *The Irish Times* in 1976 giving recollections of it – and of other animals pressed into chimney service, following an inquiry by the Irish RSPCA.

Boy begging "a noble legislator" to amend the law.

The examples chosen by Montgomery to exemplify the horrors of the boys' work enlightened many people – and they put many master-sweeps on their guard. The book was packed with information and opinion: there was a letter by a contributor, J.C. Hudson, addressed to the Mistresses of Families, whose apathy shocked him; a chapter by Mrs Alexander of York referring to the concern of members of the Society of Friends; and information about twenty and more places which had sent petitions for the prohibition of the employment of climbing boys. A copy of the Surveyor-General's report about chimney-sweeping at royal and other houses was included, together with his favourable opinion of several sweeping-machines. Other surveyors and a number of builders gave their opinion that flues could be effectually cleaned by machines, and George Smart's machine received favourable comments.

The speech which Dr Lushington had given to the Parliamentary Committee on 13 March 1818 was published at length and was supplemented by a report from St George's Hospital, to which some dying London climbing boys had been taken. James Montgomery, himself a founder-member of the Sheffield Society for Superseding the Employment of Climbing Boys, reported on the activities and investigations carried out by that Society.

Readers of Montgomery's book will have found all the information they could have wanted: authentic reports of boys' suffering and deaths, technical reports by surveyors and builders, medical reports in detail. When they turned to the Album section of the book they may not have learned anything new, but they found there a supplement to all that had gone before and a strengthening of the case for "total extirpation" of the employment. Some of the contributions to his book are included in the final chapter of this book.

Another Sheffield man was campaigning: the writer Samuel Roberts, a founder-member of the Sheffield Society. He was an early friend of the underprivileged of his day, for in 1804 he had learnt of their lives at first hand in his appointment as Overseer of the Poor, and it was his conversations with a Quaker lady, Mrs Fairbank, in 1806 which had given him his first knowledge about climbing boys. He published a book called *A Cry from the Chimneys* with an explanatory subtitle: "An Integral Part of the Total Abolition of Slavery throughout the World". The frontispiece was the picture, mentioned earlier, of the two boys who died in the bakehouse in Lothbury. Samuel Roberts dedicated his book to William Tooke, FRS, adding the words: "Success will eventually crown the persevering efforts of the righteous."

In 1837 Roberts gave a stirring lecture at a public meeting in Sheffield referring to black slaves abroad, and to enslaved children in our own country who were made black by their own work. He called out that only total extirpation of the employment would suffice, and to drive this point home he gave vivid descriptions of the boys' work: its effects, the burns, the cancer and other hardships, then told the audience of a boy whom he had found abandoned by his master; because the boy was ill he was being left to die. Roberts pressed his points home by producing a boy for the audience to look at: he was deformed, the twisted shape of his body having been caused by his work.

Roberts reminded the audience of the power of Parliament and said that the reason why the Act of 1818 had not gone through was because the House of Lords had laughed it to scorn: the Lords' laughter meant that thousands of children were consigned to misery and destruction. He quoted one of the verses of his long poem called "A Word for Climbing Boys". For a long time Roberts had had on his mind the "dirt-black, suffering, diseased, ulcerated, cancered, crippled, stunted, deformed, famished, dying poor English children".

By the time Montgomery's book came out there were a number of Societies for Superseding the Employment of Climbing Boys. The Society of Friends in York had helped to found one of the Societies in that city. The Company of Cutlers in Sheffield, which petitioned Parliament to replace the boys by machines, helped to found a Sheffield Society. The London Society, with the Duke of Sussex in the Chair, had sent a petition to Parliament to put an end to the employment of climbing boys.

It was reported in Montgomery's book that the Surveyor-General of the Board of Works recommended the use of machines, after giving reports on chimney-sweeping at royal and other houses. This would have given reassurance to the readers that the technical experts of the day were on the side of the humanitarians.

The various Societies for Superseding the Employment of Climbing Boys helped to advertise James Montgomery's *Album*, which was being published monthly by booksellers in York. The London Society paid out £10. 16s. in 1825/6 to the publishers for copies. The funds of the London Society were limited but a proportion was spent on the distribution of sweeping-machines and on encouraging the inauguration of societies throughout the country. Women, who were normally supposed to take a back seat in matters outside their homes, were encouraged to serve on the local committees.

The London Society continued to campaign for many years. They advertised the Smart sweeping-machine, and the increasing use of this led to a considerable diminution of the employment of boys in London. In 1828 the London Society advertised another machine, invented by Glass, that was an improvement on the Smart machine and was recommended by the Fire Insurance Companies.

It was not till 1834 that Parliament showed interest again.

In that year William Tooke, Hon. Treasurer of the London
Society for Superseding the Employment of Climbing
Boys, recommended that a Bill be passed to repeal the Act
of 1788. His intention was that the boys' work should be
more closely regulated by a new Act, and that none under
fourteen should be apprenticed or should climb flues to

A boy goes out from the Foundling Hospital. (The brass cap badge is
clearly showing.) Engraving by Richard Philips, 1804.

sweep them. There should be closer supervision of parish apprentices and no one should go up a burning chimney.

Members of the House of Commons were again sympathetic and added extra recommendations, such as that all boys under fourteen already employed should wear brass cap badges showing the name of their masters and the date of their indentures: a repetition of a recommendation in the 1788 Act. Penalties were to be enforced for evasion of the regulations. The construction of chimneys was to come under the regulation that they could all be cleaned by machines.

If Parliament was growing more sympathetic it can be stated that this was largely due to the growing campaign activated by the public. It was in the year 1834 that Parliament had received reports from the Select Committee, which included such members as Sir Robert Peel and Mr Tooke. The Select Committee had received petitions from all over the country, not just from the industrial north, but from Hereford, Hastings and Brighton, from Bath, Bishopwearmouth and vicinities, from Darlington and Gloucester, from Portsmouth and Tottenham and elsewhere – petitions urging Parliament to abolish the employment of climbing boys. From Bristol the Select Committee received two petitions: one for abolition, one from organized mastersweeps defending the practice. Groups of people sent petitions for abolition: such as "Clergy, Dissenting Ministers and others", and "females resident in London and vicinity".

For the Bill to go through, the sympathy of the House of Lords had to be won. After the second reading of the Bill in the Lords it was sent to Committee, with the Duke of Sutherland in the Chair. Once again evidence was heard and recorded, evidence remarkably similar to that which Jonas Hanway, David Porter and James Montgomery had already given to the public.

The Duke of Sutherland himself pointed out that there was no longer any doubt, as there had been in 1819, that machinery could clean chimneys efficiently. He instanced the 150 public buildings which were regularly swept by machinery. He made also the point that fire-insurance rates had actually fallen since machine-sweeping had been more generally adopted. Not all the Lords were persuaded of this, and some persisted in disbelieving the efficacy of machines and in showing little sympathy with the boys' physical sufferings.

A striking illustration of the way builders continued to erect chimneys which were virtually impossible to clean was in the presentation of drawings of flues in some public buildings, and in particular of the flue in the drying-room of the newly built Buckingham Palace. The evidence of Joseph Glass on this subject was important: he had invented a cleaning machine which was more flexible than the Smart apparatus, and had been well publicized by the Board of Works, by newspapers, and by Societies for Superseding the Employment of Climbing Boys. Glass had successfully cleaned all the chimneys in the House of Lords and most of Buckingham Palace – but not the drying-room flue. He maintained that a flue which could not be cleaned by machine was not fit to be cleaned by a boy.

He reported that servants were often to blame for creating difficulties over the use of machines. He emphasized, as others had done, that apertures could be made without doing damage or being unsightly, and would allow adjoining parts of the flue to be cleaned without difficulty.

The medical witness who reported to the Lords, Sir Astley Cooper, said that he must have seen a hundred cases of chimney-sweeps' cancer, leaving one to guess how many cases other doctors had treated, and how many went undiagnosed for fear of painful surgery.

Robert Steven gave impressive evidence: for years he had been in a position to collect information in his two-fold capacity of Secretary to the London Society for Superseding the Employment of Climbing Boys, and Secretary to the Hand-in-Hand Fire Office.

Tooke was asked for information. To a question about the ages of climbing boys he answered that respectable sweeps apprenticed them from eight to fourteen years, but often borrowed younger ones from each other for the narrowest flues. In the worst classes of the trade worked the youngest and most delicate children, four, five and six years of age. Tooke knew of many parents who sold their sons for three to five guineas. He reminded the committee that parents did not break the law in employing their own children at any age.

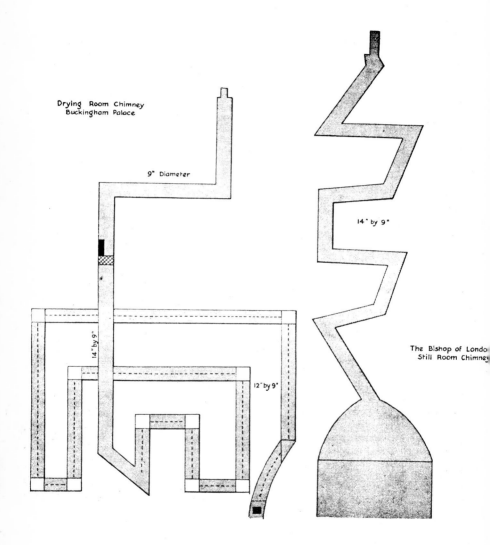

Drying Room Chimney
Buckingham Palace

9" Diameter

14" by 9"

14" by 9"

12" by 9"

The Bishop of London
Still Room Chimney

On the subject of the sweeps' trade itself, Tooke said that it was a depressed trade. There were more master-sweeps than were required and many of them had very low profits, so that their climbing boys were bound to suffer. Only the best masters sent the boys to Sunday School as enjoined by the Act, and only about twenty boys in five hundred could read and write. The despised nature of their employment, their filthy clothes, their notorious bad behaviour, cut them off from other people. Many boys reaching sixteen were virtually unemployable and many of them drifted into vice and crime.

It became clear in the course of the inquiry that the 1788 Act had become useless. Both Houses agreed to bring in a new Act and this was passed in 1834. Another milestone was reached, but not yet the final one on which the campaigners had set their sights. The regulations did, however, seem good: masters must not take on boys under the age of fourteen and not more than six apprentices at a time; boys must express themselves as willing to be apprenticed and must appear before Justices of the Peace for approval of their indentures; boys under fourteen already officially apprenticed must wear identifying cap badges on leather caps. Significant regulations were intended to ensure that apprentices would not be sent up flues to extinguish fires, or otherwise be ill-treated, nor must they be lent to other sweeps. Street-cries were regulated by this Act.

There were certain loopholes in the Act which would modify its value, and various people, including Robert Steven, protested; the Society of Master-sweeps was already organized to combat reform of their trade, and would take advantage of the loopholes. Moreover, the practice of actually climbing chimneys was not yet abolished.

The loopholes became more apparent. There were two major issues for the campaigners to contend with: the united master-sweeps' resistance to reform, and the frequently expressed statement that property would be in danger if climbing boys did not clean chimneys. But in Manchester, for example, reputable master-sweeps banded themselves against the anti-reform master-sweeps and put themselves on the side of the campaigners.

Again in 1840 a Bill was presented to Parliament. Again it was discussed and arguments for and against were repeated

— mostly the same arguments. Again the subject was referred to a Committee and the evidence of the boys' sufferings was brought forward; the reports bore a remarkable similarity to all those reports brought in evidence from 1773 onwards.

The Bill was passed and its regulations would become operative in 1842. One of the regulations was that householders must see to it that all flues were to be suitable for cleaning by machine.

This would have been a good Act if powers for enforcing it had been created. Lord Shaftesbury drew attention to its weakness by reading a report in Parliament of a ten-year-old boy's suffocation in a flue in Leeds. The master had escaped conviction because he was not present when the boy was climbing. Lord Shaftesbury's hearers will have realized this was a quibble, for what boy would climb a chimney unless instructed by a sweep? The coroner at the court, reported Lord Shaftesbury, had stated that many boys were still climbing flues, but few people reported that the law was being broken.

The branches of the Society continued their campaign, discouraged but undefeated. Here are extracts from a leaflet published in 1841 with the help and approval of the Society for Superseding the Employment of Climbing Boys. Mrs Baker, a sweep's widow, found it in her husband's papers. He had been fourth in a line of sweeps in Tunbridge Wells, his great-grandfather having founded the firm in 1814.

That from, and after the 1st day of July 1842, any person who shall compel, or knowingly allow any child or young person, under the age of twenty-one years, to ascend or descend a Chimney, or enter a flue, for the purpose of sweeping, cleaning, or coring the same; or for extinguishing fire therein, shall be liable to a penalty, not more than Ten Pounds, or less than Five Pounds. . . .

Any child apprenticed to a Chimney-sweeper may, if he is desirous, be discharged from his master, by applying to a magistrate, after the 1st day of July 1842. . . .

That from, and after the 1st day of July 1842, all existing Indentures of apprenticeship to the trade or business of a Chimney-sweeper, of any child who shall be under the age of sixteen years, shall be null and void.

For those looking for information there was nothing lacking: the four-page leaflet contained diagrammatic pictures of the boys, showing how they held their brush and moved their legs in the flues, how they passed through bends – and how a pliable machine could do the same. A right-angle turn is shown choked with soot and it is clear that an openable door fixed at the right-angle would enable the soot to be brushed away without difficulty; it is equally clear that a boy could not readily pass the heap of soot.

The publishers of the leaflet meant it to have wide circulation and they supplemented the information concerning the 1842 Act with such information as the following:

> Several accidents have occurred to boys thus employed, by their sticking fast, which is done by allowing, through inadvertence, their legs to assume the position here described; in this cramped state, children have remained hours together; but as respiration is not prevented they have been extricated alive. This position which is something like a double wedge, occurs mostly to small boys; and it has been found the more they endeavour to extricate themselves the more permanently they become fixed.

The leaflet continues with reports of children falling from stacks of chimneys to their death, or if not death, breaking bones which would incapacitate them for life. Then follows:

> Suffocation in flues has been the principal cause of death to climbing boys, which is occasioned by their passing through soot . . . which has accumulated in the angles of flues. . . . Twenty-three boys have been thus suffocated since the year 1800; in addition to which, seven have been burnt to death in chimneys (one as recently as Sunday, the 29th November 1840, in a flue of a Steam Engine, at Manchester). Fourteen others also since 1800 have in the same time lost their lives by different means, in their employment, in all forty-four.

The author of the leaflet was hopeful. Arguing that the time was fixed for "a practice so degrading and dangerous to children" to cease, he pointed out that the new carefully-designed sweeping-machine would supersede the employment of the boys. He added that the chimneys of Government Buildings, the Fire Insurance Offices, most of the Public Buildings of the Metropolis and many of the residences of the Nobility were now swept with the machines. Prices for machines with thirty-foot lengths to eighty-foot lengths are set out; they could be bought and delivered anywhere in the country. The reference to eighty-foot lengths is a reminder of the heights to which some boys were expected to climb.

Such leaflets were used to publicize the campaign to bring the employment of boys to an end. *The Penny Magazine*, founded in the thirties, was gaining a wide circulation and published informative articles about many subjects. The time for the education of the masses had come.

In the issue of 20 August 1842, three and a half columns were given to the subject of Chimneys and Chimney-Sweepers. This article touched on a number of things: the inhumanity of the employment, the neglect of scientific principles causing waste of fuel, the philanthropic schemes of Jonas Hanway, the aims of the 1800 "Society for Bettering the Condition of the Poor", the investigations by a House of Commons Committee in 1819, the 1834 Act, and so on. The article concludes: "We may perhaps look forward to the time when the cry of 'Sweep! Soot-oh!' as well as the system with which it was connected, will be reckoned among the bygone features of English life."

Other editors produced and circulated propaganda leaflets. *The Climbing Boys' Advocate* was published monthly for a while, from about 1840. The editor gave up-to-date reports on the employment of climbing boys and other matters of interest. After the 1840 Act he stated that its enactment had been of great service but had not cured the evil, adding as a concluding sentence: "The entire emancipation of the Climbing Boys mainly depends on the individual, as well as the united concurrence of a discerning public, in the resolve to dispense with their services."

In one issue of the journal two poems were published, of thirty-two lines each: one was entitled "The Climbing Boys' Appeal to the Community", the other: "The Reply to the Climbing Boys' Appeal". Four lines from each will reveal the editor's ideas:

From the "Appeal":

Our case is hard, – the lowest in degree,
Despised by others, – and ourselves not free.
We're subject to a brutal master's will,
However hard we work, he treats us ill. . . .

From the "Reply":

. . . At length – we tender what has long been due,
A list'ning ear – and deep concern for you.
. . . Thus in accordance with our earnest plea,
Announce to all, *"That Climbing Boys are free. . . ."*

So far two books have been mentioned as essential
reading from the historical point of view in the period 1773–
1875: Jonas Hanway's *Sentimental History* (1785) and James
Montgomery's *Chimney-Sweeper's Friend and Climbing-Boy's
Album* (1824). A third must be mentioned: Henry Mayhew's
London Labour and the London Poor, published in 1851 and
subsequent years. Mayhew's account of a sweep's apprenticeship has been referred to in Chapter 2.

Henry Mayhew's first title to fame is that he attended the
birth of *Punch*. This magazine, first published in 1841, had
its difficulties in getting established; it is ironic, perhaps, that
success came to this humorous journal as a result of its
publication of Thomas Hood's "Song of the Shirt", a poem
that tore the heart-strings of the Victorians. Hood wrote a
poem about chimney-sweeps' climbing boys too, but this is
in a minor key. *Punch*, the magazine of humour, has always
included the tragic and sad side of life, and climbing boys
feature in it frequently, both in picture and verse. Some
examples will be found in the last chapter.

Mayhew's second title to fame rests on the detailed
research he carried out for *London Labour and the London
Poor*. He set out to reveal to the rich and privileged something of the way of life of those who lived in deepest
poverty. He issued his writings first in twopenny numbers,
then collected them together for his book, bringing this out
in 1851. Numerous additions were made in later years. He
encouraged others to investigate the underworld of London,
adding that until others had corroborated what he reported
the readers would think he was telling travellers' tales or
fiction. He really wanted those who had not climbed the
barriers between the classes to know something of the ways

in which the lowest classes were living. He gave horrific descriptions of the slum areas which Dickens was to bring into his novels as "rookeries", and then pointed out that it was in the worst places that sweeps could be found:

> The localities in which many of the sweepers reside are the "lowest" places in the district. Many of the houses in which I found the lower class of sweepers were in a ruinous and filthy condition. . . . There are many reasons why the chimney-sweepers have ever been a distinct and peculiar class. They have long been looked down upon as the lowest order of workers, and treated with contumely by those who were but little better than themselves. The peculiar nature of their work (gives) them not only a filthy appearance, but an offensive smell, of itself, in a manner, prohibiting them from associating with other working men.

He interviewed a master-sweep of Bethnal Green, and that man's description of apprenticeship has been given in Chapter 1. His eloquence in describing a near tragedy deserves quotation; it is a true story but compares favourably with any chimney-sweep's adventures thought up by Dickens or Kingsley:

> "I had a boy once – we were called to sweep a chimney down in Poplar. When we were in, he looked up the flues.
>
> 'Well, what is it like?' I said.
>
> 'Very narrow,' he says, 'don't think I can get up there;' so after some time we gets up to the top of the house, and takes off the chimney-pot and has a look down – it was wider a' top, and I thought as how he could get down.
>
> 'You had better buff it, Jim,' says I.
>
> I suppose you know what that means; but Jim wouldn't do it, and kept his trousers on. So down he goes and gets on very well till he comes to the shoulder of the flue, and then he couldn't stir. He shouts down: 'I've stuck.' I shouts up and tells him what to do.
>
> 'Can't move,' says he. 'I'm hard and fast.'
>
> Well, the people of the house got fretted, like, but I says to them,
>
> 'Now my boy's stuck, but for Heaven's sake don't say a word, good or bad, and I'll see what I can do.'

So I locks the door and buffs it, and forces myself up till I could reach him with my hand, and as soon as he got his foot on my hand, he prises himself up, and gets loosened and comes out at the top again. I was stuck myself but I was stronger nor he, and I manages to get out again.

Now I'll be bound to say if there was another there as would kick up a row and a worrited, that there boy 'ud a niver come out of that flue alive. There was many o' them lost their lives in that way. . . ."

The reader admires the kindly sweep who not only went to the rescue of his boy but locked the door before he buffed it. He had a certain delicacy under his grime and did not want to offend the people in the house by appearing stripped and naked. At the same time he knew, and the householder should have known, that he was breaking the law by allowing a boy to climb a chimney; if he had "lost" him this fact would have come out.

In the background of the climbing boy's life there were no houses that could be counted as homes. There was no indoor or outdoor sanitation, as we know it, in the first part of the nineteenth century. How did the boys get rid of the oleaginous filth of their job? They didn't – at least for much of the time they didn't. Here are more comments from Mayhew:

In the evidence before Parliament it was stated that some of the climbing boys were washed once in six months, some once a week, some once in two or three months. I do not find it anywhere stated that any of these children were never washed at all; but from the tenor of the evidence it may be reasonably concluded that such was the case.

A master-sweeper, who was in the habit of bathing in the Marylebone baths once and sometimes twice a week, assured me that, although many now eat and drink and sleep sooty, washing is more common than when he was a climbing boy. He used then to be stripped and com-pelled to step into a tub, and into water sometimes too hot and sometimes too cold, while his mistress, to use his own words, SCOURED him. Judging from what he had seen and heard, my informant was satisfied that, from thirty to forty years ago, climbing boys, with very few exceptions, were but seldom washed, and that it was looked upon by them as a most disagreeable operation, often, indeed, as a species of punishment. Some of the climbing boys used to be taken by their masters to bathe in the Serpentine many years ago. . . .

Mayhew's reference to the Marylebone Baths is a reminder that Parliament, having acquired some knowledge about sanitation the hard way through cholera epidemics and other disasters, had passed an Act empowering local authorities to provide public baths.

Let us leave Mayhew and his book, but in doing so remind ourselves that his careful reporting and his high-lighting of many evils that needed redress helped the Victorian reformers to tackle their tasks: public cleansing for example.

Until 1847 public baths did not exist, but a Baths and Wash-houses Act was passed that year. Sir Edwin Chadwick could claim some of the credit for the passing of the Act. Writing earlier than Mayhew, this social reformer and statistician had made a great impression on people who were already terrified of cholera. "King Cholera" was pushing his kingdom out from the worst areas to the more respectable ones: the respectable people thought that they at least should be protected.

One of the first districts of London to build public baths was the parish of St Marylebone, which opened its Baths in December 1849 – only two years after the passing of the Act. The early records are interesting. The Baths consisted at first of twenty-four first-class and fifty-seven second-class baths for men, but fewer for women: six first-class and twenty second-class. Prices varied from sixpence to a penny, and the baths, particularly the cheaper ones, were much used. In its first half-century over seven million baths were taken, more than half of them being the twopenny and penny ones, for money was short. In one record week twelve thousand people took baths, the highest number in one day being as many as 3,429.

Such figures express the need for the facilities, and the appreciation of them by the working class. No doubt other growing towns could provide similar results. Indeed the midland town of Nottingham claimed to have avoided the

worst of the cholera epidemic of 1849 by its adoption of
washing and bathing facilities. The enlightened Council of
this town had been considering the need for public baths
since 1844, and, as soon as possible after the passing of the
1847 Act, went ahead with providing them. The people of
Nottingham were equally quick in taking advantage of the
facilities provided and in three months of 1851 more than
three thousand women took baths, and more than ten
thousand men: and the numbers went on increasing, a
number which "surpassed the anticipation of the most
sanguine". The clothes-washing facilities were appreciated
also, and the Council's records state that "this admirable
institution is calculated to elevate both the physical and
moral nature of the inhabitants." The Committee recorded
that they "retain their conviction that Public Baths and
Wash-houses are calculated to be of extensive benefit to the
community. Similar Institutions receive liberal support not
only in London but in Birmingham, Bristol, Hull, Liverpool, and other Towns and have recently been established in
Paris by order of the Emperor." (It is of interest to note that
the Baths and Wash-houses Committee even went so far as
to deal with smoke pollution, and in February 1854 recommended the raising of the boiler chimney by forty-five feet
to eliminate the smoke nuisance.) Those who concerned
themselves with the welfare of climbing boys in the
Nottingham area will have noted with relief that at last the
boys had facilities for regular washing.

From 1849 onwards many local authorities accepted
responsibility for the provision of public baths and wash-
houses. Thanks to such reformers as Dr Southwood Smith
and Sir Edwin Chadwick, the idea of public health began to
spread outward from London. Charles Dickens, friend of
Dr Southwood Smith, may have helped this cause as he
helped so many other causes due for reform. His literary
contributions to the campaign for the abolition of climbing
boys will be seen in the Chapter 6, but it is of significance
that he gave his personal support to practical measures of
sanitation. No one was more aware than he of the filth and
squalor in the pullulating slums of the big cities; no one had
studied more carefully the First Public Health Act (1848).

When therefore Dickens was asked by the Metropolitan
Sanitary Association to speak at their meeting on 10 May

1851 he agreed to do so. He proposed a toast to the Board of Health coupled with the name of Lord Shaftesbury, of whose services he spoke warmly. He instanced the sufferings of those people who lived where there was no water supply, he put in a plea for the poor man for whom "cleanliness must be legislated· for before godliness". Dickens's slight alteration of John Wesley's "Cleanliness is, indeed, next to godliness" will have pleased the audience forming the Metropolitan Sanitary Association. John Forster in his *Life of Charles Dickens* quotes part of his speech:

> But give him, and his, a glimpse of heaven through a little of its light and air; give them water; help them to be clean; lighten the heavy atmosphere in which their spirits flag and which makes them the callous things they are; take the body of the dead relative from the room where the living live with it, and where such loathsome familiarity deprives death itself of awe.

"Give them water; help them to be clean" might have been inscribed over all the public baths which were about to be provided. To no group of workers were these words more important than to the sweeps and their boys.

Then were sweeps and their boys admitted to the public baths, or was there a grim style of apartheid worked out? As Mayhew reported in his *London Life and the London Poor,* a master-sweep went once or twice a week to the Marylebone Baths, but other records of sweeps and their boys as customers are not easy to find. However, towards the end of the century more information is available in the Marylebone records. The committee responsible for administering the Marylebone Baths considered solemnly "as to permission being given to chimney-sweepers to use the baths at stated times, and it was resolved that the matter be left with the Superintendent to arrange". Perhaps the Superintendent had always used his discretion; it is to be hoped so. An early newspaper report stated that "one corner was pointed out for the exclusive use of sweeps, who can so comfortably and cheaply remove the honest marks of their calling and change their attire, that their own friends would hardly know them again". That reporter's reference to the "honest marks of their calling" seems to indicate that there was a growing change in attitude towards the sweep and his work: no longer does he seem to be scorned as "the lowest of the low" and his difficulties are given some sympathetic understanding.

Whether or not there was a colour bar in the public baths which were being opened in many towns from mid-century onwards, there was certainly a colour bar early on in the theatre world. In 1825 the *Morning Herald* reported that two of the London theatres agreed to admit chimney-sweepers – all other theatres being closed to them:

Astley's and the Coburg Theatres . . . are the only ones which admit chimney-sweepers in their working dress; in consequence of which, it is said that these places are sometimes honoured with this kind of sooty patronage to the extent of forty and fifty a night.

Illustration by Linley Sambourne for *The Water Babies,* 1898.

CHAPTER 4
Other Campaigners

Erected by public subscription to Anthony Ashley Cooper, K.G.,
seventh Earl of Shaftesbury, born April 28th 1801, died October
1st, 1885. During a public life of half a century he devoted the
influence of his station, the strong sympathies of his heart, and the
great powers of his mind, to honouring God by serving his fellow
men. An example to his order, a blessing to his people, and a name
to be by them ever gratefully remembered.

W.E. GLADSTONE

The above words are on "Eros", the Shaftesbury
Memorial, Piccadilly Circus, London.

1848 April 13th [following Chartist Demonstration on 10th]:
All things are tending to a change. We are entering on a new
political dispensation; and many of us probably will outlive the
integrity of our aristocratical institutions. Men are talking . . . of
"an enlargement of the franchise", and other vagaries. . . . A
Sanitary Bill would, in five years, confer more blessing and obliter-
ate more Chartism than universal suffrage in half a century.

From Lord Shaftesbury's *Diary*.

In following these writers and campaigners for social reform
we have progressed a number of years towards the year
1875 which (unknown as yet to those active in the
campaign) was to be the final milestone. It is necessary to
turn back the years to 1832 in order to give his due to the
most active and the most influential of all those who
championed the climbing boys.

The campaign needed more than books, more than
reports, more than Societies for Superseding the Employment of Climbing Boys. It needed Anthony Ashley Cooper,
known from 1851 as Lord Shaftesbury.

He concerned himself in so many matters that one can
only marvel that he was able to direct some of his energies
towards the abolition of the employment of climbing boys.
Without his concern, without his concentration, who knows
how much longer the campaign would have lasted? In *Lord
Shaftesbury* (1923) the historians J.L. and Barbara Hammond
give one chapter to summarizing the activities of this man
concerning climbing boys. If this chapter were read in iso-
lation from the rest of the book the reader would think it

Lord Shaftesbury.

was the record of a lifetime, and then would be astonished
to learn that the Hammonds could write sixteen more
chapters about Lord Shaftesbury's other commitments.

As Anthony Ashley Cooper he was appointed by Parliament adviser on child welfare in 1832. He was then thirty-
one years old. It was a pioneering post and led him into the
lives of all children who needed protection: he became the
friend of children everywhere and remained so till he died.
In Hodder's *Life of Shaftesbury* (1886) we are reminded who
these children were, in addition to the climbing boys. He
refers to:

> The unhealthy and oppressive character of the legalized
> slavery to which the childen were subjected, in connec-
> tion with employment in earthenware, porcelain, hosiery,
> pin and needle making, manufacture of arms, iron works
> and forges, iron foundries, glass trade, collieries, calico

printing, tobacco manufacture, button factories, bleaching and paper mills, and various other industries.

He devoted himself to the causes he took up. As regards the climbing boys, his work consisted not just in informing himself but in investigating for himself, in seeing boys at their work, in meeting their masters – on occasion in taking legal proceedings. In more than one case he made provision for life for those whom he rescued from a living death.

Parliament knew him well; whenever he spoke it was always with tremendous earnestness, with authentic information and with first-hand revelations. He was the prime mover, or the supporter, of many humanitarian Bills which came before Parliament from the time of his appointment concerning child welfare. It was in 1837 that he promoted the Bill which limited the labour of all children to ten hours a day.

In 1834 he had returned to the climbing boys, pleading for the "4000 wretched children who were at that time engaged in this disgusting and unnecessary employment". He stated that in Manchester sixty master-sweeps had met and testified to the degradation, cruelty, ignorance, and vice inseparable from the system, and to the readiness with which the "machines" could be effectually used, instead of climbing boys. By now, in London, machines were almost exclusively used.

Lord Shaftesbury approved of the 1840 Chimney Sweepers' Act until he found its weaknesses: it did not prevent boys from climbing, nor create good conditions of apprenticeship. He tried in 1851 and 1852 to bring in bills to strengthen the regulations. Once again, Parliament set up an inquiry and once again many reports about the conditions of employment were made. One story that emerges from the inquiry concerns Lord Beaumont, who had opposed the Bill in the House of Lords because in his opinion it was "erroneous and dangerous in principle, ineffective and miserable in detail". However, Lord Beaumont was appointed to the committee of inquiry. Peter Hall, a middle-aged sweep who had been a climbing boy at the age of seven, was questioned as to where he had seen defective chimneys. He gave Lord Beaumont's house as an example and said that the chimneys could not have been worse.

Asked when the house had been built he replied that it was in Lord Beaumont's time, and Lord Beaumont had been the architect: in other words he had disobeyed the building regulations himself. Peter Hall had a knowledge of the chimneys which no one else had, and described them as seventy feet vertical, then thirty-five feet horizontal, then sixty feet vertical. At a cost of a few shillings vents could have been inserted and the flues could have been cleaned by sweeping-machines.

In 1853 Hansard recorded Lord Shaftesbury as saying that he did not believe that all the records of all the atrocities committed, in this country or in any other, could equal the records of cruelty, hardship, vice and suffering which, under the sanction of the law, had been inflicted on this helpless and miserable race.

It was about this time that Lord Shaftesbury, ever ready to investigate bad social conditions, learned what a "lay" was. The young medical, Dr Barnardo, had reported at a meeting that he had been led on a cold night to where eleven homeless boys were sleeping rough, huddled together. Lord Shaftesbury asked Dr Barnardo to show him such a lay and subsequently the two men went together to Billingsgate by night and uncovered seventy-three young boys huddling together under a huge tarpaulin. As the number of homeless boys was legion this was not likely to be the only such lay in London. Dr Barnardo himself estimated that in the late 1870s there were some thirty thousand destitute children roaming the London streets.

In 1862 Commissioners were appointed to investigate the violation of the Chimney Sweeps' Act of 1842. The Commissioners reported that several thousand children aged between five and fourteen years, including many girls, were working for sweeps. The master-sweeps were not afraid of the law, householders connived at defiance of it, or kept themselves in ignorance of chimney-sweeping arrangements by leaving them to the domestic staff.

In 1864 Lord Shaftesbury proposed a Bill "to amend and extend the Act for the Regulation of Chimney Sweepers" and this was passed in a matter of weeks from the day in May on which he proposed it. The Act proposed stiff fines or imprisonment for sweeps violating the Act and gave the police powers to arrest sweeps thought to be breaking the law; it also gave inspectors from the Board of Health authority to inspect new or remodelled chimneys.

But all this did not amount to "total extirpation" of chimney climbing; reports continued to reach the Press about master-sweeps defying the law. As late as 1874 Hollingshead reported in his *Miscellanies* that magistrates, squires, Lords and mayors allowed their chimneys to be climbed by boys. What chance was there of convictions when sweeps were brought to court?

Lord Shaftesbury's final Bill was passed in 1875 following the much publicized death of George Brewster. This Act ensured that chimney-sweeps would be registered and that official supervision of their work would take place. Henceforth the regulations set out in earlier Acts would be carried out – and no more boys were sent up chimneys.

The remedy was after all quite "simple, obvious and certain" – just as James Montgomery had pointed out to his readers a half-century earlier.

Everything that is recorded of Lord Shaftesbury's public work reveals him as a man of exceptional sensitivity. He was ever generous in his thanks to those who supported him in his campaigns: members of Parliament and others. The opposition of those who deliberately attacked his work hurt him seriously. One of these was Lord Beaumont, who spoke of a Sweeps' Bill as "a pitiful cant of pseudo-philanthropy" and said that the 1840 Bill had been responsible for houses being burnt and lives being endangered – not, of course, the boys' lives. Lord Shaftesbury cannot have had much pleasure from the letter sent to him by Colonel Napier – who thanked him for his speech in October 1841 about the working class in general and a certain William Dodd, climbing boy, in particular, and added that he had decided to "avoid the contemplation of (the facts) in detail" as he thought he would be driven to extravagance of thought and language.

The people whom Lord Shaftesbury tried to help responded warmly to him. At a public meeting his name was mentioned and there was immediate applause from the audience. The speaker, taken by surprise, asked them what they knew of him. One man acted as spokesman:

"Know of him? Why, sir, I'm a sweep, and what did he do for me? Didn't he pass the Bill? Why, when I was a little 'un, I had to go up the chimbleys, and many a time I've come down with bleeding feet and knees, and a'most choking. And he passed the Bill as saved us from all that. That's what I know of him."

A Victorian picture which appeared after his death shows ragged, barefoot children – a sweep's boy and a shoeblack among them – laying wreaths of flowers on his memorial:

For though, say the children, he is gone,
    This is not our goodbye!
He has shown us the way to follow on,
    Till we meet him in the sky!

And the British Museum holds a picture of two diminutive shoeblacks pointing to a portrait of Lord Shaftesbury and saying: "See! That's our Lord Shaftesbury!"

The nation's memorial to Lord Shaftesbury is the statue of Eros in the middle of Piccadilly Circus, London, facing Shaftesbury Avenue. Gladstone and Shaftesbury were not always in sympathy with each other, but it is Gladstone's tribute to the reformer which is carved on the plinth of the statue and which is quoted at the opening of this chapter. A tribute of another powerful person deserves to be remembered. When Cardinal Manning finished reading Hodder's Life of Lord Shaftesbury he said: "The unity, consistency, and perseverance of his life were wonderful. He took the alleviation of human suffering and the protection of the poor and weak, as ends for which to live. He spent and was spent for it."

At the Memorial Service in Westminster Abbey over a hundred and ninety religious, charitable and other organizations sent representatives. All had a particular reason for attending the service, all had lost a personal friend. Has anyone else had such a memorial service? This great man was the best friend the climbing boy ever had.

A summary of Lord Shaftesbury's concern for the climbing boys could be made from extracts from his diaries. These were not intended for publication. He used a diary as many people do, as something to talk to in private. They reveal the Evangelical upbringing he had had and the Christian Socialism into which his religious feelings were directed. They reveal too that from time to time he succumbed to moods of deep depression – moods which probably account for periods of loss of self-confidence, as his diaries show.

Here then are some more entries from his diaries:

1840 July 4th. Anxious, very anxious, about my sweeps; the Conservative Peers threaten a fierce opposition, and the Radical Ministers warmly support the Bill. . . . I shall have no ease or pleasure in the recess, should these poor children be despised by the lords, and tossed to the mercy of their savage purchasers.

1840 August 24th. Let no one ever despair of a good cause for want of coadjutors; let him persevere, persevere, persevere, and God will raise him up friends and assistants!

1840 September 19th. Steven wrote to me yesterday, and gave me information that he had at last succeeded in negotiating the delivery of the wretched sweep behind my house in London. I had begun to negotiate, but the master stood out for more money than was fair, and we determined to see the unnatural father of the boy, and tempt him, by the offer of a gratuitous education. We have done so, and have prospered; and the child will this day be conveyed from his soothole to the Union School on Norwood Hill. . . . I entertain hopes of the boy; he is described as gentle, and of a sweet disposition; we all know he has suffered, and were eager to rescue him from his temporal and spiritual tyrant.

1847 February 25th. Time creeps on, years fly past, and the city of oppression and vice has not capitulated; the factory system stands erect; millions of infants are consumed in other departments, and, in the course of nature, it seems probable that before long I shall be removed to another scene of action – to the House of Lords. . . . In that House, except for one who holds high official station, there is little or no power of originating anything which may conduce to the welfare of the poorer sort. The Peers act as breakwaters. . . .

Then in 1854:

May 2nd. Great anxiety about Bill for relief of Chimney Sweepers. Have suffered actual tortures through solicitude for prevention of these horrid cruelties. What a mystery that our efforts have been so long unavailing.

May 20th. For three days have suffered much from giddiness and today suffer from grief. The Government in the House of Commons threw out the Chimney Sweepers' Bill, and said not a word of sympathy for the wretched children, nor of desire to amend the law. They stood on mere technicalities, Fitzroy and Lord John Russell giving the ministerial opposition. Walpole was as hostile as any of them, sacrificing the bodies and souls of thousands to a mere point of legal etiquette! . . . And again I must bow to this mysterious Providence that leaves these outcasts to their horrible destiny, and nullifies, apparently at least, all our efforts to rescue them in soul and body. (One day later) Very sad and low about the loss of the Sweeps' Bill – the prolonged sufferings, the terrible degradation, the licensed tyranny, the helpless subjection, the enormous mass of cruelty and crime on the part of parents and employers, are overwhelming.

It was at about this time that Lord Shaftesbury wondered if his influence were declining. In 1872 he wrote:

Years of oppression and cruelty have rolled on, and now a death has given me the power of one more appeal to the public through The Times. [He was referring to the death of Christopher Drummond.]

April 28th 1875. One's soul is torn, by their misery and degradation. Have prepared a Bill, the second reading stands for May 11th. God in His mercy, grace and love, be with me. . . . One hundred and two years have elapsed since the good Jonas Hanway brought the brutal iniquity before the public, yet in many parts of England and Ireland it still prevails, with the full knowledge and consent of thousands of all classes.

And then on 11 May:

Was much disheartened at outset, House very inattentive – had twice to implore their condescension to hear me. At last they listened, and so far as their undemonstrative natures would allow, applauded me. . . . Yet by his Grace I have stirred the country. The Times, may the paper be blessed, has assisted me gloriously.

The Times continued to assist: letters from Lord Shaftesbury appeared in that paper on 12 May, 4 June and 12 June.

Scattered throughout this book, from the account of Jonas Hanway onwards, are references to Christianity and the churches; Jonas Hanway, James Montgomery and many others wanted master-sweeps to be required to send their boys to church on Sundays. John Wesley (1703–91) had tried to popularize the idea that "cleanliness is next to godliness" and this idea was emphasized in apprentices' indentures which asked that master-sweeps should see that their boys had two sets of clothing and had washing facilities.

Although the various denominations of Christian churches did not make a concerted attack on the complicated problems which revealed themselves during and after the Industrial Revolution, at least individual Christians took on what they considered Christian duties towards their fellows.

This is apparent in the activities of Lord Shaftesbury, who must have been fervent in his prayers to God on behalf of the underprivileged. He confessed himself puzzled, however, by the ways of Providence when reforms were opposed. It is typical of him that when success in one of his campaigns crowned his efforts his exclamation was: "To God above be all the glory!"

Religious activity can be traced in many of the campaigners. Christian Socialism was founded and spread among churchgoers: Lord Shaftesbury shows its influence, as do Charles Kingsley and Gladstone. The Salvation Army was founded in the nineteenth century: it aimed at the spiritual, moral and social regeneration of the neediest persons, which included the climbing boys. The Moravian Church was active as a missionary force; James Montgomery was one of its members. Sunday Schools were inaugurated in 1780 by Robert Raikes (1735–1811) and they spread rapidly, providing instruction in the Christian religion as well as lessons in reading and writing.

During the hundred years and more of the climbing boys' misery, the Religious Society of Friends showed special concern for the welfare of climbing boys, as their records show. There are many instances of Friends bringing sweeps to Court for breaking the law, or of rescuing boys and educating them, or of presenting a sweeping-machine to a sweep on condition that he discharged his boy. James

Montgomery was sympathetic towards the Society of Friends, and two Quaker poets, Bernard Barton (1784–1849) and Jeremiah Wiffen (1792–1836) submitted poems for his *Album* emphasizing the plight of climbing boys. It was thought that when the numbers of climbing boys were found to be diminishing in Birmingham, Leicester, the Potteries and elsewhere, the influence of the Society of Friends was largely responsible.

Dr George Phillips,★ in carrying out his researches on the employment of English and American climbing boys, found so many references to the Society of Friends that he submitted two special articles to the Friends Historical Association which were published in 1947 and 1950. The first article opens with a report of the Quaker lady Mrs Fairbank who, as noted in chapter III, told Samuel Roberts about the degrading conditions of climbing boys' employment. Another Quaker lady, Mrs Anne Alexander of York, wrote a lengthy pamphlet about the boys, with recommendations for "the amelioration of their condition"; this was published as early as 1817 by the writer's husband, a printer.

It was characteristic of a member of the Society of Friends that Anne Alexander should encourage other Friends to concern themselves about the boys: "to assist . . . in devising means for mitigating the sorrow of these poor, oppressed children". This "concern" spread the information and it is clear from records that many members of the Society of Friends not only wrote pamphlets and newspaper articles but also helped to found and to support branches of the Society for Superseding the Employment of Climbing Boys, and to attend meetings convened by the branches.

Henry Mayhew, in his widely circulated *London Labour and the London Poor*, paid tribute to the Friends; John Hollingshead, in his "Miscellanies" of 1874, also praised them, pointing out that most of the prosecutions were instigated either by master-sweeps who used machines, or by members of the Society of Friends.

In the second half of the nineteenth century another

★ Dr George Phillips. Some of the information about the Society of Friends in this chapter is taken from Dr Phillips's articles with his permission.

member of a family of the Society of Friends concerned herself with climbing boys: Mrs Sewell (1797–1884) asked her friends for donations towards a sweeping-machine for the sweep she employed, and she saw to it that he accepted the machine and used it instead of using boys. Like her famous daughter Anna, Mrs Sewell was a writer. She wrote sympathetically of the hardships of the poor, and, urging practical action, said: "We do not want societies. We want individual kindness. I have no objection whatever to kind-hearted ladies having their working-parties and sending frocks, handkerchiefs and flannel petticoats to the black populations but let them first see to their poor neighbours." Charles Dickens, it will be remembered, created Mrs Jellyby to personify this style of misplaced philanthropy.

Mrs Sewell's brother, John Wright, was as practical as his sister. When he visited, in 1867, the reformatory at Buxton where a nephew was in charge, he found that a master-sweep had come to collect an apprentice. Parents of other boys in the reformatory objected to their sons being apprenticed, but one boy had no friends or relations and would have been selected; John Wright stepped in and prevented the boy from being taken.

The Times on 11 March 1868 referred in an obituary notice to the philanthropic work of William Wood (1782–1868): he had worked untiringly for the climbing boys and was one of those who had taken master-sweeps to court and had befriended their unfortunate apprentices.

Concern spread to Ireland and energetic activities within the Society of Friends were evident there. From 1838 to 1840 articles about the boys were published in *The Irish Friend,* a monthly periodical. "J.C." wrote suggesting that householders should buy Glass's machine and hire men – not sweeps – to clean their chimneys with it. One writer, signing himself "N", paid tribute to two of the other contributors because their articles had persuaded him to make a study of the little sweeps' conditions.

Climbing boys were employed in the United States, and more of this will be discussed in Chapter 5. There too the concern of Friends showed itself. Roberts Vaux, a Friend living in Philadelphia, wrote to William Dillwyn of Walthamstow about Smart's machine. An extract from the letter was published in *The Times* on 5 August 1818:

And I take pleasure in assuring thee of its introduction here with every prospect of soon removing from this employment to better service those unfortunate and unpitied little black children, who have so long excited the notice of some of our citizens, travelling our streets in tattered garments during the most severe weather of our climate.

The climbing boys were doubtless unaware of the religious stirrings that were taking place. It is unlikely that they knew of the long-drawn-out campaign that was waged on their behalf, nor of the proliferation of charitable organizations in the nineteenth century. It is worth remembering all these as this chapter on the campaigners comes to an end, because they reveal the new social conscience which was to ensure the continuing concern for children's welfare in the twentieth century.

CHAPTER 5
American Climbing Boys

In America, what were pickaninnies for, if not to climb chimnies?
Who would buy a machine so long as there were plenty of cheap
boys?
PROFESSOR JOHN HURD,
Introduction to *American Chimney Sweeps* (1957)

The system inherited from England flourished so long as boys were
economic assets in the trade.
PROFESSOR GEORGE LEWIS PHILLIPS,
American Chimney Sweeps (1957)

If Chimneys were more frequently and more carefully clean'd some
Fires might thereby be prevented. I have known foul Chimneys
burn most furiously a few Days after they were swept: People in
Confidence that they are clean, making large Fires. . . . Those who
undertake Sweeping of Chimneys and employ servants for that
Purpose, ought to be licensed by the Mayor; and if any Chimney
fires and flames out 15 Days after Sweeping, the Fine should be
paid by the Sweeper; for it is his Fault.
BENJAMIN FRANKLIN, in
The Pennsylvania Gazette, 4 February 1734

What has happened in other countries? Is Great Britain the
only country to provide a black record about chimney-
sweeping? There is little to report of boys climbing
chimneys in Europe, although it is known that boys were
employed in France and Italy, indeed some English boys
were deported to clean chimneys in France. Austria and
Germany have an honourable record, chimney-sweeps
taking a pride in their work and having no recourse to
climbing boys.

The World History of Sweeps which Dr George Phillips,
former Professor of English Literature at San Diego State
College, was preparing for many years has not been completed: his work was interrupted when, ironically enough,
the ever-present danger of fire revealed itself. While he and
his wife were away on holiday, fire swept through their
bungalow at La Mesa, California. Much of a great collection of books, historical records, and "sweepiana" – his
word for a collection of sweeps' mementoes – was seriously
damaged; repair work proved time-consuming, and compi-

lation of his book was postponed indefinitely. The fire took place in 1977, when Dr Phillips was already a septuagenarian.

It was an early contribution of Dr Phillips to *The Dickensian* which introduced me to him: I read his article, "Dickens and the Climbing Boys" (1953) twenty years after he had written it. It was Charles Lamb's essay "In Praise of Chimney-Sweepers" which had first stirred his interest – a good link in the literary chain between the two English-speaking countries, a link which would have pleased the compassionate heart of Elia.

Although Dr Phillips will not now publish a comprehensive history of chimney-sweeps, he has already written two carefully researched books for limited circulation: *England's Climbing Boys: a History of the Long Struggle to Abolish Child Labor in Chimney-Sweeping* (Boston, 1949) and *American Chimney Sweeps* (New Jersey, 1957).

Research led Dr Phillips to his reading numerous state documents, literary references, old newspapers, and, as John Hurd has said, "running halfway over London to secure the accuracy of just one fact. . .". The flyleaf of my copy of *American Chimney Sweeps* is inscribed: "To Fellow Sweepo-phile with Sweeps' Luck in Her Investigation of the sooty men and boys."

One paragraph in the Introduction to this book provides a summary which reads remarkably like a summary of our English story. After referring to Dr Phillips's travels to American and European libraries for his research, Professor John Hurd states that the book is about:

> Sweeps' . . . costumes and sleeping quarters, their school-ing and food, their apprenticeships and their owners (the boys were in effect slaves), their deformities and diseases (most often tuberculosis of the lungs and cancer of the scrotum), their chants when they emerged from chimney tops, the crusades against exploitation of child labor in the chimneys and the prolonged refusals by Parliament to alleviate the lot of the emaciated waifs.

He adds a personal comment: "For these puny outcasts Professor Phillips has a large and generous compassion with exact scholarship."

So what is the history of the American climbing boys? In sum there seems to be a close parallel between the situations in Britain and America, but some aspects are different. From the seventeenth century onwards American public authorities attempted to supervise and control chimney-sweeping. Early houses in America were mostly an invitation to fire, for their structures consisted largely of logs and boarding, planks and thatch. The houses were built at close quarters, not because of demands on space, but because the inhabitants were thus seeking protection against Indian raids. If a fire started in one house it spread quickly to the adjoining wooden structures.

Fires were frequent and devastating. In the eighteenth century in those places where there were no self-employed sweeps to carry out the essential work the municipal authorities attempted to appoint sweeps. Other authorities drew up regulations for the construction of flues and the roofing of houses, and tried to enforce them. Others again imposed fines on house-owners if their chimneys caught fire – fines which were often impossible to pay. In some places building inspectors and fire wardens were appointed.

Methods of sweeping were similar to those in England: for a wide short flue a long-handled broom could be used, the sweep or house-owner standing on a ladder and sweeping from above. In a narrow flue a bundle of bricks in a bag, or bundles of brushwood, were dropped down a chimney to dislodge the soot to the floor-level. In flues deemed climbable a thin boy was forced to go up, sometimes encouraged by pins in feet or buttocks, or by straw-firing on the hearth. In order to avoid penalties some householders devised their own methods of clearing their chimneys; some of them – perhaps hearing of English and Irish geese which had been sent down chimneys – tried out the method of sweeping-by-geese. Luckily for the birds this practice proved to be so objectionable that most people gave it up. News of the sweeping-machine invented by Smart in 1803 travelled across the Atlantic, but only in limited numbers were they taken on. In the next two decades numerous inventors applied for patents for their sweeping-machines.

As in England the chimney-sweeping trade acquired a stigma: this was totally undeserved in view of the importance of the work. The stigma had an adverse effect on the future of the trade. During the eighteenth century the employment of coloured sweeps spread northwards from the south, and as Negroes, slave or free, became involved, so the white men and boys gave up the trade which society despised so much. Dr Phillips's book contains a number of pictures, one of them a reproduction of a water-colour (1811) showing a chimney-sweep with two ill-clad boys on a street in Philadelphia; the other an early photograph (1848) of five young slaves from South Carolina. The author comments:

. . . The tragic history of American chimney sweeps concerns not merely white boys turned sooty in color, and as in England, forced into slavery but that in this country, unlike any other, the noisome work was forced on boys born black and blackened still further by the debasement arising from race stigma and the debasement arising from exploitation of human beings brought to the Land of the Free. . . .

As in England, also, the training of the boys was minimal: how could a boy be *trained* to sweep a chimney? Forced to climb it, brush and scraper in hand, he had to evolve his own technique for scrambling up the narrow flue, rubbing elbows and knees on the sooty flue walls; no master-sweep could teach the boy after he disappeared up the chimney.

Coloured men and boys did not prove more efficient than whites, and householders disliked them, blaming them in particular for loss of property caused by fires, and claiming that there was more destruction by fire in New York than in London. The actual climbing of a chimney flue in America and of one in Britain must have been similar; no doubt master-sweeps in the two countries resembled each other – some humane but most of them not, some of them ready to learn the use of sweeping-machines but most of them preferring boys, some of them law-abiding, some of them deliberately and successfully defiant of the law: the climbing boy was a human brush, and it was the work of the brush that was important not the boy himself: he was expendable. In both countries compassionate people were to be found showing concern for sweeps' boys.

Occupational hazards in America have been recorded as resembling the all too familiar English ones: American climbing boys did not escape death by suffocation, nor by falling from a height if the chimney stack gave way, nor by severe burns when the flue was too hot. They did not escape severe accidents nor those occupational illnesses which have already been mentioned: blear eyes caused by soot under the eyelids, lung illnesses caused by breathing it, cancer caused by the soot on the unwashed skin of the scrotum, ulcerous sores on knees and elbows. In 1937 Dr Sidney Henry of England sent to the *American Journal of Cancer* his "Study of Fatal Cases of Cancer of the scrotum 1911–1935 with special reference to chimney sweeping and cotton-mule spinning".

Organizations that sprang up in England did not repeat themselves in America – such as the branches of the Society for Superseding the Employment of Climbing Boys; nor did the American literary world concern itself so much about the boys as did the nineteenth-century English novelists, poets and essayists and journalists, although American street cries, numerous ballads, and occasional stories are recorded.

There is one book, however, which deserves mention: *Tit for Tat*, published in 1854. The author was "A Lady from New Orleans" and her compassion for the climbing boys was matched by her anger at England's hypocrisy in concerning herself with slaves in America and disregarding – according to the author – white children "fettered to British Chimneys". "Tit" was the climbing boy of England, "Tat" the Negro slave in the south; the novel was a popular one in America and created sympathy for the boys. The author's anger was perhaps roused again when she learned that her book was not so widely read as *Uncle Tom's Cabin* by Harriet Beecher Stowe: first published in 1850, it crossed the Atlantic and did much to influence British public opinion about the slave trade.

Some quotations from Dr Phillips's book *American Chimney Sweeps* show that his researches into American sources resemble in many details those made in Great Britain:

> So impressed was one kind-hearted person at the sight of a decently garbed colored master sweep who fed his apprentices well, dressed them warmly in cold weather, and accompanied them to church on Sundays, that he insisted: "This man should be encouraged. . . . House-holders should look out for this man and praise him."

Evidently the onlooker had seen plenty of the other kind of master-sweep.

Then their sleeping habits:

> Sweep-boys, especially those working for the poorer masters who hired them from their owners, enjoyed few comforts. If, after sleeping black (i.e. unwashed) for months, they felt the need to rid their bodies of dirt and vermin, they could jump into a river. . . . The boys slept huddled closely together on piles of straw in the cellar or shed where the soot was piled and drew over them the sere, often holey, blankets that they tacked over the mantels to keep the soot from entering a room. Their food was often broken victuals handed them by the cooks in the houses where they went to work. . . . The young sweeps, as shown in contemporary illustrations, seem to have snatched their ragged garments from scarecrows in the cornfields. . . .

Their early morning habits:

> Even before dawn in winter the labors of the boys began as they left their lodgings, munching, if they were fortunate, a dry crust of bread. Shrilly they cried the streets for work, incurring the householders' wrath. . . . Punctual though they might be to undertake their work, they often were obliged to stand shivering in the snow or rain until a disgusted servant huddled on some clothes and grumpily admitted them.

Their afternoon leisure:

> Usually, the sweep boys did not work beyond noon; consequently, they had some free time. Many of them, imitating their masters, threw dice and wandered about the streets in a rowdy manner. An article on juvenile disorders in the "National Standard" (Middlebury, Vermont) for February 27, 1821, commented on the youths of staid Middlebury thronging the streets "hooting and howling, savage-like, and in imitation of the licentious cow-boys and sooty chimney-sweeps in the suburbs of an ill-regulated city".

Eventually, towards the end of the nineteenth century, there was one last boy employed to climb chimneys, one last chimney climbed, allowing American humanitarians, like their English counterparts, to divert their attention to other social problems.

And today, towards the end of the twentieth century? The young people who sweep chimneys today – chimneys for the new type of fuel – are not dirty, undersized, deformed: they have developed a new style of cleaning chimneys and wear clean clothes to work in. They have been to school and college, they are intelligent, their work is lucrative and appreciated, they organize their own unions and publish their own news-sheets. To mark the changes, they have changed their name: they are fluonomists. Sweeps' proverbial luck has, it would seem, caught up with the "fluonomists": the story of the climbing boy in America, as in England, came to an end a century ago.

"The Land of the Free" is an expression beloved in both the countries and it can be read between the lines throughout Dr Phillips's book as clearly as in the poems and prose collected for the next chapter.

CHAPTER 6
Climbing Boys in Art and Literature

The little chimney-sweeper skulks along
And marks with sooty stains the heedless throng. . . .
JOHN GAY, *Trivia* (1716)

In adding the album section to his *Chimney-Sweeper's Friend and Climbing Boy's Album* James Montgomery showed shrewd intuition. He saw that factual reports and philanthropic pleas might not suffice to win over the public at large. In the long struggle to free the climbing boys, creative writers of the calibre of Blake, Lamb and Dickens did much to establish a climate of opinion conducive to reform.

This chapter includes a selection from the original *Album* but adds a great deal of material never available to Montgomery, who would have been appalled to know how long the fight he entered would have to continue. The main purpose of this collage is to suggest how powerfully the chimney-boys intrigued and troubled the society which produced them. Conspicuous to the eye in their symbolic blackness and to the ear through their shrill cries of advertisement, they haunted our streets for more than a century, rousing pity and moral unease. Their strange craft and unique appearance attracted speculation and became the stuff of legend: the soot might hide some kidnapped princeling. Their prominence in the chimney-sweepers' May Day celebrations associated them with folklore and superstition. In their poverty, drudgery and contagious dirtiness, they became apt subjects for indignant didactic verse or cautionary tales for children.

The extracts included here reach beyond the nineteenth century to show how long the picturesque image of the poor chimney-boy remained vivid in the public mind.

THE CHIMNEY SWEEPER

When my mother died I was very young,
And my father sold me while yet my tongue
Could scarcely cry "'weep! 'weep! 'weep! 'weep!"
So your chimneys I sweep, & in soot I sleep.

There's little Tom Dacre, who cried when his head,
That curl'd like a lamb's back, was shav'd: so I said
"Hush, Tom! never mind it, for when your head's bare
"You know that the soot cannot spoil your white hair."

And so he was quiet, & that very night,
As Tom was a-sleeping, he had such a sight!
That thousands of sweepers, Dick, Joe, Ned & Jack,
Were all of them lock'd up in coffins of black.

And by came an Angel who had a bright key,
And he open'd the coffins & set them all free;
Then down a green plain leaping, laughing, they run,
And wash in a river, and shine in the Sun.

Then naked & white, all their bags left behind,
They rise upon clouds and sport in the wind;
And the Angel told Tom, if he'd be a good boy,
He'd have God for his father, & never want joy.

And so Tom awoke; and we rose in the dark,
And got with our bags & our brushes to work.
Tho' the morning was cold, Tom was happy & warm;
So if all do their duty they need not fear harm.

WILLIAM BLAKE (1757–1827), *Songs of Innocence* (1789)

Sweep's boy.

THE CHIMNEY SWEEPER

A little black thing among the snow,
Crying "'weep! 'weep!" in notes of woe!
"Where are thy father & mother, say?"
"They are both gone up to the church to pray.

"Because I was happy upon the heath,
"And smil'd among the winter's snow,
"They clothed me in the clothes of death,
"And taught me to sing the notes of woe.

"And because I am happy & dance & sing,
"They think they have done me no injury,
"And are gone to praise God & his priest & King,
"Who make up a heaven of our misery."

WILLIAM BLAKE (1757–1827), *Songs of Experience* (1794)

I wander through each charter'd street,
Near where the charter'd Thames doth flow,
And mark in every face I meet
Marks of weakness, marks of woe.

In ev'ry cry of every Man,
In ev'ry Infant's cry of fear,
In every voice, in every ban,
The mind-forged manacles I hear.

Now the Chimney Sweeper's cry
Every black'ning Church appals:
And the hapless Soldier's sigh
Runs in blood down palace walls. . . .

WILLIAM BLAKE (1757–1827)

From the diary of Sophie de la Roche. The entry was made when she visited London.

September 6, 1786 — As however the maids seldom open their eyes before eight o'clock, I was already dressed when I saw the first workman passing and heard a young voice calling: "Chimney-sweep! chimney-sweep!" and perceived a tiny chimney-sweep boy, six years old, running along barefoot at his master's side, his soot-bag on his back, and shouting for all he was worth.

SOPHIE DE LA ROCHE

THE LITTLE SWEEP

They sing of the poor sailor-boy who wanders o'er the deep,
But few are they who think upon the friendless LITTLE
    SWEEP.
In darkness to his dreary toil, through winter's frost and
    snows,
When the keen north is piping shrill, the shivering urchin
    goes.

He has no father, and from grief his mother's eyes are dim,
And none besides, in all the world, awakes to pray for HIM:
For him no summer Sunday smile, no health is in the breeze;
His mind dark as his fate, his frame a prey to dire disease.

Oh! English gentlemen! your hearts have bled for the black
    slave,
You heard his melancholy moan from the Atlantic wave;
He thought upon his father's land, and cried, "A LONG
    FAREWELL,"
But bless'd you, gazing at the sun when first his fetters fell.

And if ye plead for creatures dumb, and deem their fate
    severe,
Shall *human wrongs,* in *your own* land, call forth no generous
    tear?
Humanity implores! Awake from apathy's cold sleep!
And when you plead for others' wrongs, forget not the
    poor SWEEP.

When summer comes the bells shall ring, and flowers and
    hawthorns blow,
The village lasses and the lads shall all "a–Maying" go:
Kind hearted Lady, may thy soul in heaven a blessing reap,
Whose bounty at that season flows, to cheer the LITTLE
    SWEEP.

'Tis yours, ye English Gentlemen, such comforts to prolong;
'Tis yours the friendless to protect, and all who suffer wrong.
But one day in the toiling year the friendless sweep is gay,
Protect, – and smiling industry shall make his long year
    MAY!

THE REV. F. LISLE BOWLES (1760–1852)

Boy following master on a donkey.
(Drawing by Phoebe Sholto–Douglas)

(Trade card.)

THE CHIMNEY SWEEPER

"Sweep! sweep! sweep! sweep!" cries little Jack,
With brush and bag upon his back,
   And black from head to foot;
While daily, as he goes along,
"Sweep! sweep! sweep! sweep!" is all his song
   Beneath his load of soot.

But then he was not always black,
Oh, no! he once was pretty Jack,
   And had a kind Papa;
But, silly child! he ran to play
Too far from home, a long, long way,
   And did not ask Mamma.

So he was lost, and now must creep
Up chimneys, crying "Sweep! sweep! sweep!"

ELIZABETH TURNER, *The Daisy* (1806)

THE LAWYER AND THE CHIMNEY-SWEEPER

A roguish old lawer was planning new sin,
  As he lay on his bed in a fit of the gout;
The maids and the daylight were just coming in,
  The milkmaids and rush-lights were just going out;

When a chimney-sweep's boy, who had made a mistake,
  Came flop down the flue with a clattering rush,
And bawl'd, as he gave his black muzzle a shake,
  "My master's a-coming to give you a brush."

"If that be the case," said the cunning old elf,
  "There's no time to lose – it is high time to flee –
Ere he gives me a brush, I will brush off myself –
  If I wait for the devil – the devil take me!"

So he limp'd to the door without saying his pray'rs;
  But Old Nick was too deep to be nick'd of his prey;
For the knave broke his neck by a tumble down stairs,
  And thus ran to the devil by running away.

ANON

Illustration by Linley Sambourne for *The Water Babies,* 1898.

The last Chimney Sweeper.

A large brush made of a number of small whalebone sticks, fastened into a round ball of wood, and extending in most cases to a diameter of two feet, is thrust up the chimney by means of hollow cylinders or tubes, fitting into one another like the joints of a fishing rod, with a long cord running through them; it is worked up and down, as each fresh joint is added, until it reaches the chimney pot; it is then shortened joint by joint, and on each joint being removed, is in like manner worked up and down in its descent; and thus yon have your chimney swept perfectly clean by this machine, which is called a Scandiscope.

> Some wooden tubes, a brush, and rope,
> Are all you need employ;
> Pray order, maids, the Scandiscope,
> And not the climbing boy.

Copy of a printed hand-bill, distributed before May-day, 1826.

The "Scandiscope" sweeps rejoice because climbing chimneys will be abolished.

IN PRAISE OF CHIMNEY-SWEEPERS

I like to meet a sweep – understand me – not a grown
sweeper – old chimney-sweepers are by no means attractive
– but one of those tender novices, blooming through their
first nigritude, the maternal washings not quite effaced from
the cheek – such as come forth with the dawn, or somewhat
earlier, with their little professional notes sounding like the
peep peep of a young sparrow; or liker to the matin lark
should I pronounce them, in their aerial ascents not seldom
anticipating the sun-rise?

I have a kindly yearning towards these dim specks – poor
blots – innocent blacknesses –

I reverence these young Africans of our own growth –
these almost clergy imps, who sport their cloth without
assumption; and from their little pulpits (the tops of
chimneys), in the nipping air of a December morning,
preach a lesson of patience to mankind.

When a child, what a mysterious pleasure it was to
witness their operation! to see a chit no bigger than one's
self enter, one knew not by what process, into what seemed
the *fauces Averni* – to pursue him in imagination, as he went
sounding on through so many dark stifling caverns, horrid
shades! – to shudder with the idea that "now, surely, he
must be lost for ever!" – to revive at hearing his feeble shout
of discovered daylight – and then (O fullness of delight)
running out of doors, to come just in time to see the sable
phenomenon emerge in safety, the brandished weapon of
his art victorious like some flag waved over a conquered
citadel! I seem to remember having been told, that a bad
sweep was once left in a stack with his brush, to indicate
which way the wind blew. It was an awful spectacle certainly; not much unlike the old stage direction in Macbeth,
where the "Apparition of child crowned with a tree in his
hand rises".

Reader, if thou meetest one of these small gentry in thy
early rambles, it is good to give him a penny. It is better to
give him twopence. If it be starving weather, and to the
proper troubles of his hard occupation, a pair of kibed heels
(no unusual accompaniment) be superadded, the demand on
thy humanity will surely rise to a tester. . . .

I am by nature extremely susceptible of street affronts; the jeers and taunts of the populace; the low-bred triumph they display over the casual trip, or splashed stocking, of a gentleman. Yet can I endure the jocularity of a young sweep with something more than forgiveness. In the last winter but one, pacing along Cheapside with my accustomed precipitation when I walk westward, a treacherous slide brought me upon my back in an instant. I scrambled up with pain and shame enough – yet outwardly trying to face it down, as if nothing had happened – when the roguish grin of one of these young wits encountered me. There he stood, pointing me out with his dusky finger to the mob, and to a poor woman (I suppose his mother) in particular, till the tears for the exquisiteness of the fun (so he thought it) worked themselves out at the corners of his poor red eyes, red from many a previous weeping, and soot-inflamed, yet twinkling through all with such a joy, snatched out of desolation, that Hogarth – but Hogarth has got him already (how could he miss him?) in the March to Finchley, grinning at the pie-man – there he stood, as he stands in the picture, irremovable, as if the jest was to last for ever – with such a maximum of glee, and minimum of mischief, in his mirth – for the grin of a genuine sweep hath absolutely no malice in it – that I could have been content, if the honour of a gentleman might endure it, to have remained his butt and his mockery till midnight.

I am by theory obdurate to the seductiveness of what are called a fine set of teeth. Every pair of rosy lips (the ladies must pardon me) is a casket presumably holding such jewels; but, methinks, they should take leave to "air" them as frugally as possible. The fine lady, or fine gentleman, who show me their teeth, show me bones. Yet must I confess, that from the mouth of a true sweep a display (even to ostentation) of those white and shining ossifications, strikes me as an agreeable anomaly in manners, and an allowable piece of foppery. It is as when

"A sable cloud
Turns forth her silver lining on the night."

It is like some remnant of gentry not quite extinct; a badge of better days; a hint of nobility: – and, doubtless, under the obscuring darkness and double night of their forlorn dis-

guisement, oftentimes lurketh good blood, and gentle conditions, derived from lost ancestry, and a lapsed pedigree.
The premature apprenticements of these tender victims give
but too much encouragement, I fear, to clandestine, and
almost infantile abductions; the seeds of civility and true
courtesy, so often discernible in these young grafts (not
otherwise to be accounted for) plainly hint at some forced
adoptions; many noble Rachels mourning for their children,
even in our days, countenance the fact; the tales of fairy-
spiriting may shadow a lamentable verity, and the recovery
of the young Montagu be but a solitary instance of good
fortune, out of many irreparable and hopeless *defiliations.*

In one of the state-beds at Arundel Castle, a few years
since – under a ducal canopy – (that seat of the Howards is
an object of curiosity to visitors, chiefly for its beds, in
which the late Duke was especially a connoisseur) – en-
circled with curtains of delicatest crimson, with starry
coronets inwoven – folded between a pair of sheets whiter
and softer than the lap where Venus lulled Ascanius – was
discovered by chance, after all methods of search had failed,
at noonday, fast asleep, a lost chimney-sweeper. The little
creature, having somehow confounded his passage among
the intricacies of those lordly chimneys, by some unknown
aperture had alighted upon this magnificent chamber; and,
tired with his tedious explorations, was unable to resist the
delicious invitement to repose, which he there saw
exhibited; so, creeping between the sheets very quietly, laid
his black head upon the pillow, and slept like a young
Howard.

Such is the account given to the visitors at the Castle. –
But I cannot help seeming to perceive a confirmation of
what I have just hinted at in this story. A high instinct was
at work in the case, or I am mistaken. Is it probable that a
poor child of that description, with whatever weariness he
might be visited, would have ventured, under such a
penalty as he would be taught to expect, to uncover the
sheets of a Duke's bed, and deliberately to lay himself down
between them, when the rug, or the carpet, presented an
obvious couch, still far above his pretensions – is this
probable, I would ask, if the great power of nature, which I
contend for, had not been manifested within him,
prompting to the adventure? Doubtless this young noble-

man (for such my mind misgives me that he must be) was allured by some memory, not amounting to full consciousness, of his condition in infancy, when he was used to be lapt by his mother, or his nurse, in just such sheets as he there found, into which he was now but creeping back as into his proper *incunabula,* and resting-place. — By no other theory, than by this sentiment of a pre-existent state (as I may call it), can I explain a deed so venturous, and indeed, upon any other system, so indecorous, in this tender, but unseasonable, sleeper.

My pleasant friend JEM WHITE was so impressed with a belief of metamorphoses like this frequently taking place, that in some sort to reverse the wrongs of fortune in these poor changelings, he instituted an annual feast of chimney-sweepers, at which it was his pleasure to officiate as host and waiter. It was a solemn supper held in Smithfield, upon the yearly return of the fair of St Bartholomew. Cards were issued a week before to the master-sweeps in and about the metropolis, confining the invitation to their younger fry. Now and then an elderly stripling would get in among us, and be good-naturedly winked at; but our main body were infantry. One unfortunate wight, indeed, who, relying upon his dusky suit, had intruded himself into our party, but by tokens was providentially discovered in time to be no chimney-sweeper (all is not soot which looks so), was quoited out of the presence with universal indignation, as not having on the wedding garment; but in general the greatest harmony prevailed. The place chosen was a convenient spot among the pens, at the north side of the fair, not so far distant as to be impervious to the agreeable hubbub of that vanity; but remote enough not to be obvious to the interruption of every gaping spectator in it. The guests assembled about seven. In those little temporary parlours three tables were spread with napery, not so fine as substantial, and at every board a comely hostess presided with her pan of hissing sausages. The nostrils of the young rogues dilated at the savour. JAMES WHITE, as head waiter, had charge of the first table; and myself, with our trusty companion BIGOD, ordinarily ministered to the other two. There was clambering and jostling, you may be sure, who should get at the first table – for Rochester in his maddest days could not have done the humours of the scene

with more spirit than my friend. After some general
expression of thanks for the honour the company had done
him, his inaugural ceremony was to clasp the greasy waist
of old dame Ursula (the fattest of the three), that stood
frying and fretting, half-blessing, half-cursing "the gentleman," and imprint upon her chaste lips a tender salute,
whereat the universal host would set up a shout that tore the
conclave, while hundreds of grinning teeth startled the night
with their brightness. O it was a pleasure to see the sable
younkers lick in the unctuous meat, with *his* more unctuous
sayings – how he would fit the tit-bits to the puny mouths,
reserving the lengthier links for the seniors – how he would
intercept a morsel even in the jaws of some young desper-
ado, declaring it "must to the pan again to be browned, for
it was not fit for a gentleman's eating" – how he would
recommend this slice of white bread, or that piece of
kissing-crust, to a tender juvenile, advising them all to have
a care of cracking their teeth, which were their best
patrimony, – how genteelly he would deal about the small
ale, as if it were wine, naming the brewer, and protesting, if
it were not good, he should lose their custom; with a special
recommendation to wipe the lip before drinking. Then we
had our toasts – "The King", – the "Cloth", – which,
whether they understood or not, was equally diverting and
flattering; – and for a crowning sentiment, which never
failed, "May the Brush supersede the Laurel." All these, and
fifty other fancies, which were rather felt than compre-
hended by his guests, would he utter, standing upon tables,
and prefacing every sentiment with a "Gentlemen, give me
leave to propose so and so", which was a prodigious
comfort to those young orphans; every now and then
stuffing into his mouth (for it did not do to be squeamish on
these occasions) indiscriminate pieces of those reeking
sausages, which pleased him mightily, and was the
savouriest part, you may believe, of the entertainment.

"Golden lads and lasses must,
As chimney-sweepers, come to dust."

James White is extinct, and with him these suppers have
long ceased. He carried away with him half the fun of the
world when he died – of my world at least. His old clients
look for him along the pens; and missing him, reproach the

altered feast of St Bartholomew, and the glory of Smithfield departed for ever.

CHARLES LAMB (1775–1834)

"The Sweep's House"

A large party are invited to dinner – a great display is to be made – and about half an hour before dinner there is an alarm that the kitchen chimney is on fire! It is impossible to put off the distinguished personages who are expected. It gets very late for the soup and fish, the cook is frantic – all eyes are turned upon the sable consolation of the master chimney-sweeper – and up into the midst of the burning chimney is sent one of the miserable little infants of the brush! There is a positive prohibition of this practice; and an enactment of penalties in one of the Acts of Parliament which respects chimney-sweepers. But what matter Acts of Parliament, when the pleasures of genteel people are concerned? Or what is a toasted child, compared to the agonies of the mistress of the house with a deranged dinner?

THE REV. SYDNEY SMITH (1771–1845),
in *The Edinburgh Review*

THE STREETS — MORNING

Here and there, a bricklayer's labourer, with the day's dinner tied up in a handkerchief, walks briskly to his work, and occasionally a little knot of three or four schoolboys on a stolen bathing expedition rattle merrily over the pavement, their boisterous mirth contrasting forcibly with the demeanour of the little sweep, who, having knocked and rung till his arm aches, and being interdicted by a merciful legislature from endangering his lungs by calling out, sits patiently down on the door-step until the housemaid may happen to awake.

CHARLES DICKENS (1812–70),
Sketches by Boz (1836)

The Streets, Morning *George Cruikshank*

Another immortal picture of London is: 'Early Morning' by
George Cruikshank. The scene is a coffee stall beside a
London lamp-post. A little chimney sweep and his master
are on their way to work, and have stopped for breakfast.
The rest of London is sleeping. . . . The heart of Cruikshank, I
have no doubt, was touched by the plight of the poor little
boy, as black as the soot he worked in, and probably sold into
bondage from the workhouse. . . . In its small way, this small
etching is a wonderful and eternal work of art.

SACHEVERELL SITWELL (1897–   )
Truffle Hunt with Sacheverell Sitwell, 1953

Illustration by Isaac Cruikshank (c.1756–1811) of a group of over-dressed dandies in a shop; a sweep's boy jeers at them for their pinched-in waists, his own garments providing a striking contrast.

THE FIRST OF MAY

We remember, in our young days, a little sweep about our own age, with curly hair and white teeth, whom we devoutly and sincerely believed to be the lost son and heir of some illustrious personage – an impression which was resolved into an unchangeable conviction on our infant mind, by the subject of our speculations informing us, one day, in reply to our question, propounded a few moments before his ascent to the summit of the kitchen chimney, "that he believed he'd been born in the vurkis, but he'd never know'd his father". We felt certain from that time forth that he would one day be owned by a lord, at least;

A pickpocket in custody.
Illustration by George Cruikshank from *Sketches by Boz*.

and we never heard the church-bells ring, or saw a flag
hoisted in the neighbourhood, without thinking that the
happy event had at last occurred, and that his long-lost
parent had arrived in a coach and six, to take him home to
Grosvenor-square. He never came, however; and, at the
present moment, the young gentleman in question is settled
down as a master sweep in the neighbourhood of Battle-
bridge, his distinguishing characteristics being a decided
antipathy to washing himself, and the possession of a pair of
legs very inadequate to the support of his unwieldy and
corpulent body. . . .

This gradual decay and disuse of the practice of leading
noble youths into captivity, and compelling them to ascend
chimneys, was a severe blow, if we may so speak, to the

Appearing in public.
Illustration by George Cruikshank from *Memoirs of Joseph Grimaldi*.

romance of chimney-sweeping, and to the romance of spring at the same time. But even this was not all, for some years ago the dancing on May-day began to decline; small sweeps were observed to congregate in twos or threes, unsupported by a "green", with no "My Lord" to act as master of the ceremonies, and no "My Lady" to preside over the exchequer. Even in companies where there was a "green" it was an absolute nothing – a mere sprout; and the instrumental accompaniments rarely extended beyond the shovels and a set of Pan-pipes, better known to the many, as a "mouth-organ".

The First of May.
Illustration by George Cruikshank from *Sketches by Boz*.

These were signs of the times, portentous omens of a coming change; and what was the result which they shadowed forth? Why, the master sweeps, influenced by a restless spirit of innovation, actually interposed their authority, in opposition to the dancing, and substituted a dinner – an anniversary dinner at White Conduit House – where clean faces appeared in lieu of black ones smeared with rose pink; and knee cords and tops superseded nankeen drawers and rosetted shoes.

Gentlemen who were in the habit of riding shy horses; and steady-going people, who have no vagrancy in their souls, lauded this alteration to the skies, and the conduct of the master sweeps was described as beyond the reach of praise. But how stands the real fact? Let any man deny, if he can, that when the cloth had been removed, fresh pots and

The pugnacious cabman.
Illustration by Phiz for *Pickwick Papers*.

pipes laid upon the table, and the customary loyal and patriotic toasts proposed, the celebrated Mr Sluffen, of Adam-and-Eve court, whose authority not the most malignant of our opponents can call in question, expressed himself in a manner following: "That now he'd cotcht the cheerman's hi, he vished he might be jolly vell blessed, if he worn't a goin' to have his innings, vich he would say these here obserwashuns – that how some mischeevus coves as know'd nuffin about the consarn, had tried to sit people agin the mas'r swips, and take the shine out o' their bis'nes, and the bread out o' the traps o' their preshus kids, by a makin' o' this here remark, as chimblies could be as vell svept by 'sheenery as by boys; and that the makin' use o' boys for that there purpuss vos barbareous; vereas, he 'ad been a chummy – he begged the cheerman's parding for usin' such a wulgar hexpression – more nor thirty year – he might say he'd been born in a chimbley, and he know'd uncommon vell as 'sheenery vos vus nor o' no use: and as to kerhewelty to the boys, everybody in the chimbley line know'd as vell as he did, that they liked the climbin' better nor nuffin as vos." From this day, we date the total fall of the last lingering remnant of May-day dancing, among the *élite* of the profession: and from this period we commence a new era in that portion of our spring associations which relates to the 1st of May.

CHARLES DICKENS (1812–70),
in *Sketches by Boz* (1836)

Mr Swiveller's pugilistic skill.
Illustration by Phiz for *The Old Curiosity Shop*.

It chanced one morning, while Oliver's affairs were in this auspicious and comfortable state, that Mr Gamfield, chimney-sweep, went his way down the High Street, deeply cogitating in his mind his ways and means of paying certain arrears of rent, for which his landlord had become rather pressing. Mr Gamfield's most sanguine estimate of his finances could not raise them within full five pounds of the desired amount; and, in a species of arithmetical desperation, he was alternately cudgelling his brains and his donkey, when, passing the workhouse, his eyes encounterd the bill on the gate.

"Wo-o!" said Mr Gamfield to the donkey.

The donkey was in a state of profound abstraction: wondering, probably, whether he was destined to be regaled with a cabbage-stalk or two when he had disposed of the two sacks of soot with which the little cart was laden; so, without noticing the word of command, he jogged onward.

Mr Gamfield growled a fierce imprecation on the donkey generally, but more particularly on his eyes; and, running after him, bestowed a blow on his head, which would inevitably have beaten in any skull but a donkey's. Then, catching hold of the bridle, he gave his jaw a sharp wrench, by way of gentle reminder that he was not his own master; and by these means turned him round. He then gave him another blow on the head, just to stun him till he came back again. Having completed these arrangements, he walked up to the gate, to read the bill.

The gentleman with the white waistcoat was standing at the gate with his hands behind him, after having delivered himself of some profound sentiments in the boardroom. Having witnessed the little dispute between Mr Gamfield and the donkey, he smiled joyously when that person came to read the bill, for he saw at once that Mr Gamfield was exactly the sort of master Oliver Twist wanted. Mr Gamfield smiled, too, as he perused the document; for the five pounds was just the sum he had been wishing for; and, as to the boy with which it was encumbered, Mr Gamfield, knowing what the dietary of the workhouse was, well knew he would be a nice small pattern, just the very thing for register stoves. So, he spelt the bill through again, from beginning to end; and then, touching his fur cap in token of

Oliver escapes being bound apprentice to the Sweep.

humility, accosted the gentleman in the white waistcoat.

"This here boy, sir, wot the parish wants to 'prentis," said Mr Gamfield.

"Ay, my man," said the gentleman in the white waistcoat, with a condescending smile. "What of him?"

"If the parish vould like him to learn a right pleasant trade, in a good 'spectable chimbley-sweepin' bisness," said Mr Gamfield, "I wants a 'prentis, and I am ready to take him."

"Walk in," said the gentleman in the white waistcoat. Mr

Gamfield having lingered behind, to give the donkey another blow on the head, and another wrench of the jaw, as a caution not to run away in his absence, followed the gentleman with the white waistcoat into the room where Oliver had first seen him.

"It's a nasty trade," said Mr Limbkins, when Gamfield had again stated his wish.

"Young boys have been smothered in chimneys before now," said another gentleman.

"That's acause they damped the straw afore they lit it in the chimbley to make 'em come down agin," said Gamfield; "that's all smoke, and no blaze; vereas smoke ain't o' no use at all in making a boy come down, for it only sinds him to sleep, and that's wot he likes. Boys is wery obstinit, and wery lazy, gen'lmen, and there's nothink like a good hot blaze to make 'em come down vith a run. It's humane too, gen'lmen, acause, even if they've stuck in the chimbley, roasting their feet makes 'em struggle to hextricate theirselves."

The gentleman in the white waistcoat appeared very much amused by this explanation; but his mirth was speedily checked by a look from Mr Limbkins. The board then proceeded to converse among themselves for a few minutes, but in so low a tone, that the words "saving of expenditure", "looked well in the accounts", "have a printed report published", were alone audible. These only chanced to be heard, indeed, on account of their being very frequently repeated with great emphasis.

At length the whispering ceased; and the members of the board having resumed their seats and their solemnity, Mr Limbkins said:

"We have considered your proposition, and we don't approve of it."

"Not at all," said the gentleman in the white waistcoat.

"Decidedly not," added the other members.

As Mr Gamfield did happen to labour under the slight imputation of having bruised three or four boys to death already, it occurred to him that the board had, perhaps, in some unaccountable freak, taken it into their heads that this extraneous circumstance ought to influence their proceedings. It was very unlike their general mode of doing business, if they had; but still, as he had no particular wish to revive the rumour, he twisted his cap in his hands, and walked slowly from the table.

"So you won't let me have him, gen'lmen?" said Mr Gamfield, pausing near the door.

"No," replied Mr Limbkins; "at least, as it's a nasty business, we think you ought to take something less than the premium we offered."

Mr Gamfield's countenance brightened, as, with a quick step, he returned to the table, and said,

"What'll you give, gen'lmen? Come! Don't be too hard on a poor man. What'll you give?"

"I should say, three pound ten was plenty," said Mr Limbkins.

"Ten shillings too much," said the gentleman in the white waistcoat.

"Come!" said Gamfield; "say four pound, gen'lmen. Say four pound, and you've got rid on him for good and all. There!"

"Three pound ten," repeated Mr Limbkins, firmly.

"Come! I'll split the difference, gen'lmen," urged Gamfield. "Three pound fifteen."

"Not a farthing more," was the firm reply of Mr Limbkins.

"You're desperate hard upon me, gen'lmen," said Gamfield, wavering.

"Pooh! pooh! nonsense!" said the gentleman in the white waistcoat. "He'd be cheap with nothing at all, as a premium. Take him, you silly fellow! He's just the boy for you. He wants the stick, now and then: it'll do him good; and his board needn't come very expensive, for he hasn't been overfed since he was born. Ha! ha! ha!"

Mr Gamfield gave an arch look at the faces round the table, and, observing a smile on all of them, gradually broke into a smile himself. The bargain was made. Mr Bumble was at once instructed that Oliver Twist and his indentures were to be conveyed before the magistrate, for signature and approval, that very afternoon.

CHARLES DICKENS (1812–70),
Oliver Twist (1838), Chapter III

Illustration by Phiz for *Dombey & Son*.

"Grimes rode the donkey in front and Tom and the brushes walked behind." Illustration by W. Heath Robinson for *The Water Babies*.

Once upon a time there was a little chimney-sweep, and his name was Tom. That is a short name, and you have heard it before, so you will not have much trouble in remembering it. He lived in a great town in the North country, where there were plenty of chimneys to sweep, and plenty of money for Tom to earn and his master to spend. He could not read nor write, and did not care to do either; and he never washed himself, for there was no water up the court where he lived. He had never been taught to say his prayers. He never had heard of God, or of Christ, except in words which you never have heard, and which it would have been well if he had never heard. He cried half his time, and laughed the other half. He cried when he had to climb the dark flues, rubbing his poor knees and elbows raw; and when the soot got into his eyes, which it did every day in the week; and when his master beat him, which he did every day in the week; and when he had not enough to eat, which happened every day in the week likewise. And he laughed the other half of the day, when he was tossing halfpennies with the other boys, or playing leapfrog over the posts, or bowling stones at the horses' legs as they trotted by, which last was excellent fun, when there was a wall at hand behind which to hide. As for chimney-sweeping, and being hungry, and being beaten, he took all that for the way of the world, like the rain and snow and thunder, and stood manfully with his back to it till it was over, as his old donkey did to a hail-storm; and then shook his ears and was as jolly as ever; and thought of the fine times coming, when he would be a man, and a master sweep, and sit in the public-house with a quart of beer and a long pipe, and play cards for silver money, and wear velveteens and ankle-jacks, and keep a white bull-dog with one grey ear, and carry her puppies in his pocket, just like a man. And he would have apprentices, one, two, three, if he could. How he would bully them, and knock them about, just as his master did to him; and make them carry home the soot sacks, while he rode before them on his donkey, with a pipe in his mouth and a flower in his button-hole, like a king at the head of his army. Yes, there were good times coming; and, when his master let him have a pull at the leavings of his beer, Tom was the jolliest boy in the whole town.

CHARLES KINGSLEY (1819–75),
The Water Babies (1863), Chapter I

Cover of *Eversley and Bramshill Parish Magazine*.
Illustration for *The Water Babies*.

GEORGE AND THE CHIMNEY SWEEP

His petticoats now George cast off
  For he was four years old;
His trousers were of nankeen stuff,
  With buttons bright as gold.
"May I," said George, "just go abroad,
  My pretty clothes to show?
May I, mamma? but speak the word;"
  The answer was: "No, no."

"Go run below, George, in the court,
  But go not in the street,
Lest boys with you should make some sport
  Or gipsies you should meet."
Yet tho' forbidden, he went out,
  That other boys might spy,
And proudly there he walked about,
  And thought – "How fine am I!"

But whilst he strutted through the street,
  With looks both vain and pert,
A sweep-boy passed, whom not to meet
  He slipped – into the dirt.
The sooty lad, whose heart was kind,
  To help him quickly ran,
And grasp'd his arm with "Never mind,
  You're up, my little man."

Sweep wiped his clothes with labour vain,
  And begged him not to cry.
And when he'd blackened every stain,
  Said "Little sir, goodbye."
Poor George, almost as dark as sweep,
  And smeared in dress and face,
Bemoans with sobs, both loud and deep,
  His well-deserved disgrace.

JANE and ANN TAYLOR (1782–1846 and 1783–1866)

EXCELSIOR

Some few, whose days are closing fast,
Remember in their time long past,
How youth, in toil of little price,
Might yet have borne, for their device, Excelsior!

Those youngsters, in that distant time,
Swept chimneys, which they had to climb.
They could have cried as they climbed higher,
Like one who skywards did aspire, Excelsior!

Our "Climbing Boys", as they were called,
Howe'er they "Sweep!" and "Soot O!" bawled,
As they ascended up the flue
Were not instructed to halloo Excelsior!

By reek and close air overcome,
The Climbing Boys were oft struck dumb,
And stifled soon unless got out –
Of course he then no more could shout Excelsior!

His knees were worn by rough ascent
Bare to the very ligament;
Flayed were his fingers and his toes,
Because he grazed them as he rose Excelsior!

When, jammed in, on his upward way
He stuck fast, oft, some used to say,
His master, in the grate below,
Would light a fire, to make him go Excelsior!

These horrors having been at last
Dragged into day, an Act was passed
Declaring it, henceforth, a crime
To make a child a chimney climb Excelsior!

Still certain Bumbles, it appears,
Against the law, these many years,
Have had their Town Hall's chimneys swept
By means of little boys who crept Excelsior!

May a new law, more strictly framed,
All parties hit at whom 'tis aimed,
Concerned in making children sweep
Foul flues, whilst painfully they creep Excelsior!

Long brush worked deftly by machine,
All chimneys must be Bumbles, clean.
Law must on cruel masters fall,
Who take to driving urchins small – Excelsior!

PERCIVAL LEIGH (*Punch*, 1875)

PROGRESS OF CIVILISATION.

Ramoneur (*on Donkey*). "Fitch us out another Pen'north o' Strawberry Ice,
with a Dollop of Lemon Water in it."

"SEE! THAT'S OUR LORD SHAFTESBURY!"

Illustration by William McDuff from *The Ragged School Union Quarterly Record*, 1878.

Sir – The valuable letter from Mr Hawker in your impression of yesterday states amply and clearly the evil and the remedy in the case of climbing boys.

There is no flue in all Great Britain and Ireland which might not be made accessible to the sweeping machine, at the expense of a few shillings in most instances, and of a few pounds in the remainder. This has been well proved by the extirpation of the climbing system in London, with its four millions of inhabitants, and in Glasgow, with its half-million. . . .

It is simply monstrous that, to suit the parsimony, the indolence, or the obstinacy of proprietors, magistrates, and master-sweepers, this inhumane and degrading servitude should be permitted, by connivance, in this age and country.

Meanwhile, what are the School Boards about, with their compulsory power? . . . All these lads are under 13 years of age. I never was an admirer of these institutions, but I remember urging in the House of Lords that they would, at least, be the means of checking the wicked and cruel perversion of infant life, to the service of acrobats, chimney-sweepers, and low pantomimes.

With many thanks for the support you have ever given to this cause,

I am, Sir, your obedient servant. . . .

Lord Shaftesbury, *The Times*, March 1875

"Have you really the courage to go out into the wide world with me?" asked the chimney-sweeper. "Have you reflected how large it is, and that we can never come back hither?"

"I have," she said.

And the chimney-sweeper looked hard at her, and said: "My way lies through the chimney. Have you really the courage to go with me, not only through the stove itself, but to creep through the flue? We shall then come out by the chimney, and then I know how to manage. We shall climb so high that they won't be able to reach us, and quite at the top is a hole that leads out into the wide world."

And he led her to the door of the stove.

"It looks very black," said she: still, in she went with him, both through the stove and through the pipe, where it was as dark as pitch.

"Now we are in the chimney," said he; "and look! there shines the most beautiful star above!"

And it was a real star in the sky that seemed to shine down upon them as though it would light them on their way. And now they climbed and crept, and a frightful way it was – so steep and so high! But he went first, and smoothed it as much as he could; he held her, and showed her the best places to set her little china foot upon, and so they managed to reach the edge of the chimney-pot, on which they sat down – for they were vastly tired, as may be imagined.

The sky and all its stars was above them, and all the roofs of the town lay below. They saw far around them, and a great way out into the wide world.

HANS CHRISTIAN ANDERSEN (1805–75),
from *The Chimney Sweep and the China Shepherdess*

Brass plaque of Hans Andersen's *Chimney Sweep and China Shepherdess.*

Mr. Soot the Sweep

Master Soot the Sweep's Son.

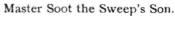

Mr. Soot the Sweep

Master Soot the Sweep's Son.

Mrs. Soot the Sweep's Wife

Miss Soot the Sweep's Daughter

SOOT

SOOT

Mrs. Soot the Sweep's Wife

Miss Soot the Sweep's Daughter

Cards from "Happy Families" by Sir John Tenniel.

SOOEEP!

Black as a chimney is his face,
  And ivory white his teeth,
And in his brass-bound cart he rides,
  The chestnut blooms beneath.

"Sooeep, sooeep!" he cries, and brightly peers
  This way and that, to see
With his two light-blue shining eyes
  What custom there may be.

And once inside the house, he'll squat,
  And drive his rods on high,
Till twirls his sudden sooty brush
  Against the morning sky.

Then 'mid his bulging bags of soot,
  With half the world asleep,
His small cart wheels him off again,
  Still hoarsely bawling "Soeep!"

WALTER DE LA MARE (1873–1956),
Peacock Pie (1913)

THE CHIMNEY-SWEEP.

I reverence these young Africans of our own growth—who from their little pulpits (the tops of chimnies) in the nipping air of a December morning preach a lesson of patience to mankind.

ESSAYS OF ELIA.

Sweep! Sweep!
Saddle your donkey and set on your way!
There's chimneys need sweeping at Iken today.
Bring brushes and scrapers and baskets and sacks
To harvest the soot from our chim-in-ey stacks.

Black Bob is coming and with him his lad,
A sullen apprentice as black as his Dad,
Their cries as they ride through the sharp morning air
Set partridges drumming and startle the hare.

Sam is the white boy, and sweep is his job,
His father has sold him to cruel Black Bob.
Today is his black day: today he must climb
A chim-in-ey stack for the very first time.

Snape lies behind them, and over the bridge
They strike to the left by a narrowing ridge;
Then follow the wandering dyke where it leads
Through thickets of rushes and tussocks of reeds.

ERIC CROZIER, libretto from Benjamin Britten's
"The Little Sweep" in *Let's Make an Opera* (1949)

Producing a sensation, from *The Old Curiosity Shop*.

And he who gives a child a treat
Makes joy-bells ring in Heaven's street
And he who gives a child a home
Builds palaces in Kingdom Come.

JOHN MASEFIELD (1878–1967), Poet Laureate,
The Everlasting Mercy

Social reformers: postage stamps designed by David Gentleman, 1976.

CONCLUSION

It was the record of a death of a climbing boy in 1822 which first caught my attention and made me want to find out more about sweeps' apprentices. It is the death of the last climbing boy in 1875 which has fixed the final date of importance in this book. My parents and grandparents were alive when George Brewster made his way into history by way of the chimney flue in Fulbourn Hospital.

The relative nearness in time brings home to us the extraordinary changes which have taken place in our way of life since the period covered by this book, in particular the changes in our attitude to children.

"What's the point?" the sweep asked me, when I said I was learning a lot about climbing boys. "Plenty of other hardships for children when those boys were climbing chimneys; forget it, it's the present and future that we need to think about."

"What *is* the point?" I ask myself; and I realize that this book is concerned with children in relation to society. The story of the climbing boy is so hideous that we have to turn away from it and thank goodness that it is over. This need not stop us from asking if the problems for young childen are now in a fair way to being solved. Can the conscience of the public allow itself to stop pricking?

Already there were kindly people in Valentine Gray's day – in Tom's day – in George Brewster's day. They came out of seclusion to rescue "suffering innocence". Influential people campaigned on behalf of the little victims of the industrial revolution. *The Times* earned the nickname of "The Thunderer" for its thunder against social evils; other papers spread information to those who were willing to accept it.

Nowadays societies to help children are proliferating. They are a natural development from the nineteenth century, when organizations were already being formed; their foundations have proved to be solid enough to last until today.

Nowadays, too, class barriers are getting shaky: they have

become easier to climb over, easier to knock down or ignore. A volume of *Punch* of a hundred years ago has pictures of overdressed, refined little boys and girls whose world does not touch the world of guttersnipes and climbing boys and cockney urchins – the world into which Dr Barnardo took Lord Shaftesbury one night.

Since I made the acquaintance of Valentine Gray I find that he and the other boys often come into my thoughts. When I have a hot bath I think of what the expression "sleeping black" meant. When I visit stately homes and admire the architecture, the hearths and chimney stacks, I think of the boys who shinned up the flues – along the straight bits where the soot accumulated, along the bewildering branches, up the vertical lengths. When I read novels or biographies of the middle and upper classes of the Victorian era I am aware of the shadowy people in the background, grown-ups and children of the lower class, who enabled them to live in comfort.

How would the campaigners against the employment of climbing boys view the position of children today? They would see a network of social workers throughout the country; among the services they carry out is a caring service for all children in need. Supplementary to the statutory services are the voluntary organizations which concentrate on some special aspect of child welfare. The Welfare State has set up a social security organization which aims to give every family freedom from hunger, from poverty and from homelessness. The medical services are expanding their medical care of children and carrying out more and more research on children's illnesses and accidents. Education of children has been compulsory since 1870 and nowadays is subjected to so much publicity that all parents must be aware of the aims and objects and methods of the educators on behalf of the children. There are enforceable regulations concerned with the employment of children.

All this and more the campaigners would discover. Then like my friend the sweep they would remind us that it is the present and the future which matter and I think I hear them stressing the importance of having the needs of children constantly in mind.

A HIGH TREAT.

THE FELLOW STUDENTS.

INDEX

Wilson, Ann, 27
Wood, William, 86
Woodforde, Parson, 32
World History of Sweeps (Phillips), 88
Wright, John, 86

Wright, Richard, 49, 50
Wyer, William, 31, 32

"XYZ", 25, 26

Young, T., 27